Whoever Controls the Schools Rules the World

Gary DeMar

AMERICAN VISION
POWDER SPRINGS, GEORGIA

A M E R I C A N   V I S I O N

A BIBLICAL WORLDVIEW MINISTRY

THE MISSION OF AMERICAN VISION, INC. IS TO PUBLISH AND DISTRIBUTE BOOKS THAT LEAD INDIVIDUALS TOWARD:

A personal faith in the one true God: Father, Son, and Holy Spirit

A lifestyle of practical discipleship

A worldview that is consistent with the Bible

An ability to apply the Bible to all of life

Copyright © 2007 Gary DeMar.

Published January 2007

First Edition

Second Printing June 2007

Printed in the United States of America

No part of this publication may be reproduced, stored in a retrieval system, or transmitted in any form by any means, electronic, mechanical, photocopy, recording, or otherwise, without the prior written permission of the publisher, except for brief quotations in critical reviews and articles.

Unless otherwise noted, all Scripture quotations are from the New American Standard Version of the Bible.

Cover design: Luis Lovelace

Typesetting: James DeMar

American Vision, Inc.
3150-A Florence Road
Powder Springs, Georgia 30127-5385
www.americanvision.org
1–800–628–9460

Library of Congress Cataloging-in-Publication Data

DeMar, Gary,

    Whoever Controls the Schools Rules the World / Gary DeMar—1st ed.

    ISBN 0–915815–64–8

    1. Education 2. Civilization, Western 3. Religion and science

This book is dedicated to Dr. Ellsworth McIntyre and the staff members of Grace Community Schools, Naples, Florida.

Table of Contents

Introduction

WHOEVER CLAIMS SOVEREIGNTY[1] expects his subjects to govern his realm in terms of his name and law. Sovereignty, therefore, brings with it the inevitability of control.[2] The beast of Revelation 13 claimed absolute sovereignty when he required his subjects to operate in terms of his law and name.

> And he causes all, the small and the great, and the rich and the poor, and the free men and the slaves, to be given a mark on their right hand, or on their forehead, and he provides that no one should be able to buy or sell, except the one who has the mark, either the name of the beast or the number of his name (Rev. 13:16–17).[3]

The Lamb, the true sovereign, expects sovereignty to be exercised in His name (14:1–5). All others are usurpers and competitors.

The denial of one sovereign assumes the sovereignty of another. There are no exceptions. If God is denied as the only true and independent sovereign, man will claim this attribute for himself. For example, when Jerusalem was plundered by Nebuchadnezzar and his army, certain young men were brought to Babylon "to enter the king's personal service," that is, to further the kingdom of Babylon (Dan. 1:5). This was partly accomplished through education. Keep in mind that *religion* was at the foundation of it all. First came the plundering of the old religion, the introduction of the new sovereign, and finally capturing the best and the brightest to be indoctrinated into the ways of the new religion controlled by the State (1:1). The prevailing religion of a nation determines the educational curriculum as controlled by the civil magistrate.

To symbolize the change in sovereignty, new names were given to these young sons of Judah. The names of Daniel, Hananiah, Mishael, and Azariah reflected the majesty and sovereignty of the God of Israel. The suffixes of their names reflect either the general name for God (*el*) or a form of His personal name (*yah*). Daniel means *God is my judge*. Hananiah means *Jehovah has favored*. Mishael can be translated *Who is what God is?* Azariah means *Jehovah has helped*. In each case, Babylonian names were substituted that reflected the attributes of the Babylonian gods, Marduk and Nebo. Babylonian religion remains a potent force in American public education as humanist John Dunphy makes clear:

> I am convinced that the battle for humankind's future must be waged and won in the public school classroom by teachers who correctly perceive their role as the proselytizers of a new faith: a religion of humanity that recognizes and respects the spark of what theologians call divinity in every human being. These teachers must embody the same selfless dedication as the most rabid fundamentalist preachers, for they will be ministers of another sort, utilizing a classroom instead of a pulpit to convey humanist values in whatever subject they teach, regardless of the educational level—preschool day care or large state university. The classroom must and will become an arena of conflict between the old and the new—the rotting corpse of Christianity, together with all its adjacent evils and misery, and the new faith of humanism, resplendent in its promise of a world in which the never-realized Christian ideal of "love thy neighbor" will be finally achieved.[4]

The goals of the humanists are clear and forthright. They hide nothing and demand everything. The humanist agenda has been relentless in its efforts to remake man and the world in the image of autonomous man. There is no compromise or lack of vision on their part. The humanist worldview is comprehensive. A concerted and planned effort has been made by humanist thinkers to "capture the robes"[5] of society by working for an ideological monopoly in the areas of education, law, science, and religion. For too long, Christians have believed that an arena of neutrality and immunity exists where humanists and Christians can discuss issues based on an "objective" study of the facts. Unfortunately, the humanists never adopted the neutrality myth while they sold it to us at a very high price. While Christians have been sold the spoiled goods of neutrality, fair play, objectivity, toleration, and pluralism, the humanists have been promoting and implementing their worldview in every area of life while denying what they tell us we should believe. It's unfortunate that many Christians still believe that neutrality is possible and that humanists strive to pursue objectivity in education. Nothing could be further from the truth. All facts are interpreted facts, and humanists want them interpreted without any regard for God and His Word.

Contrary opinions regarding the facts are not considered. The State has determined what the standard will be to interpret the facts. The humanists have understood this for a long time, so they made it their business to capture the robes of civil government so they could control the means of perpetuating their worldview. Humanist social theory has turned education into a god, a god that they now control. Laws are written and legislation enacted, all in the name of the misreading of the First Amendment, to shut out all rival religions. Taxes—civil government's tithe (1 Sam. 8)—are paid to the State in support of the State church: schools. Rousas J. Rushdoony has described the process as *The Messianic Character of American Education.*[6] Consider the ruling of the Ninth Circuit Court on what role parents have in the education of their own children once they are in the hands of state educators:

> Parents have a right to inform their children when and as they wish on the subject of sex; they have no constitutional right, however, to prevent a public school from providing its students with whatever information it wishes to provide, sexual or otherwise, when and as the school determines that it is appropriate to do so. Neither *Meyer* nor *Pierce* [two earlier Supreme Court

rulings] provides support for the view that parents have a right to
prevent a school from providing any kind of information—sexual
or otherwise—to its students.... Perhaps the Sixth Circuit said it
best when it explained, "While parents may have a fundamental
right to decide *whether* to send their child to a public school, they
do not have a fundamental right generally to direct *how* a public
school teaches their child."[7]

There you have it. The State, through the agency of the courts, has declared
that it is the sovereign ruler over your child's education. Did you notice how
the court describes the relationship between your children and the schools
they attend in the use of the phrase "*its* children"? They are *your* children.
Will you continue to allow your children to be indoctrinated in what is an
ungodly educational system, or will you make the choice, while you still
can, to put them in an educational setting where the God of the Bible is
recognized as the true sovereign? The decision remains with you.

Notes

1. "Supreme power; supremacy; the possession of the highest power, or of uncontrollable power. Absolute *sovereignty* belongs to God alone." (Noah Webster, *American Dictionary of the English Language* [1828]).

2. The biblical system of government is decentralized, therefore, its control factor is not concentrated in any one individual, group, institution, or civil jurisdiction.

3. Revelation has often been interpreted as referring to events that are still in our future. A number of commentators hold the position that Revelation was written prior to the destruction of Jerusalem in A.D. 70 and the beast of Revelation 13 is a first-century figure. For a study of Revelation, see Steve Gregg, *Revelation: Four Views—A Parallel Commentary* (Nashville, TN: Thomas Nelson, 1997).

4. Quoted in John W. Whitehead, *Stealing of America* (Westchester, IL: Crossway Books, 1983), 95.

5. Robes are a symbol of authority in the West. Three groups wear robes to identify their profession and as an indication that each profession has been invested with a degree of formal authority: judges, university professors, and ordained ministers.

6. Rousas J. Rushdoony, *The Messianic Character of American Education: Studies in the History of the Philosophy of Education* (Philadelphia, PA: Presbyterian and Reformed, 1963).

7. Stephen Reinhardt, Ninth Circuit Court of Appeals, *Opinion: Fields v. Palmdale* (Nov. 2, 2005), 14–15. Available online at http://caselaw.lp.findlaw.com/data2/circs/9th/0356499p.pdf

Part I

1

A Modern History of Educational Control

"One of the most useful tools in the quest for power is the educational system."[1]

THE SIGNIFICANCE OF the above quotation is self-evident: Whoever controls the educational system will set the goals for the nation, define and establish its moral values, and ultimately rule the future in every area of life. Children and the worldview they embrace are the future. Much can be learned from a study of the historical record of social movements and political regimes that have made their goal to extinguish any glowing ember of a Christian worldview.

The Third Reich

Many of Adolf Hitler's atrocities are well known because of their heinous character and thorough documentation. Because of this, many philosophical or *worldview* atrocities get little notice when compared with the violent images that have shaped our understanding of Nazism. Nazism destroyed body, mind, and soul. By capturing the youth through education, Adolph Hitler believed that his dreams of a Nazi State could be realized. In *Mein Kampf,* Hitler stressed "the importance of winning over and then training the youth in the service 'of a new national state.'"[2] His words and subsequent actions were a prelude to understanding what the world would have been like had he succeeded. William L. Shirer, an eyewitness to the rise of Hitler and the Nazi worldview, offers an objective but chilling prospect of what was in store for Europe and possibly the world:

> "When an opponent declares, 'I will not come over to your side,' [Hitler] said in a speech on November 6, 1933, "I calmly say, 'Your child belongs to us already . . . What are you? You will pass on. Your descendants, however, now stand in the new camp. In a short time they will know nothing else but this new community.'" And on May 1, 1937, he declared, "This new Reich will give its youth to no one, but will itself take youth and give to youth its own education and its own upbringing."[3]

Educational control was taken away from parents and local authorities and "Every person in the teaching profession, from kindergarten through the universities, was compelled to join the National Socialist Teachers' League which, by law, was held 'responsible for the execution of the ideological and political co-ordination of all the teachers in accordance with the National Socialist doctrine.'"[4] The State was to be supported "without reservation" and teachers took an oath to "be loyal and obedient to Adolf Hitler."[5]

The nation that birthed the Reformation and made the Bible the center of all that was right and good was now swearing allegiance to a new savior. "Heil Hitler" became the public declaration that the voice of Hitler, like that of Herod nearly two millennia before him, was perceived to be "the voice of a god and not a man" (Acts 13:23).

Nazism is a comprehensive ideology that sees no boundaries or exclusions. Hitler's goal was to remake the social, cultural, political, educational, and moral climate of his day in the image of the Nazi worldview. "In Germany there was Nazi truth, a Nazi political truth, a Nazi economic truth, a Nazi social truth, a Nazi religious truth, to which all institutions had to subscribe or be banished."[6] All competing worldviews were expunged from the State educational curriculum. Neutrality was never an option for Hitler. In fact, neutrality is not even possible. Not to take a side is to acquiesce to the competition.[7]

Christianity's Destruction

Religion was not exempt from the plotting Hitler. Under the leadership of Alfred Rosenberg, an outspoken pagan and anti-Christian, "the Nazi regime intended eventually to destroy Christianity in Germany."[8] Martin "Bormann, one of the men closest to Hitler, said publicly in 1941, 'National Socialism and Christianity are irreconcilable.'"[9] While we hear a great deal about the suppression of Jewish thought, little attention is given to Nazism's most formidable rival—Christianity. War correspondent Shirer wrote, "We know now what Hitler envisioned for the German Christians: the utter suppression of their religion."[10] The internal intelligence agency of the Nazi SS "regarded organized Christianity as one of the major obstacles to the establishment of a truly totalitarian state."[11]

When Martin Niemoeller used his pulpit to expose Hitler's radical politics and its comprehensive worldview implications, "He knew every word spoken was reported by Nazi spies and secret agents."[12] Leo Stein describes in his book *I Was in Hell with Niemoeller* how the Gestapo gathered evidence against Niemoeller:

> Now, the charge against Niemoeller was based entirely on his sermons, which the Gestapo agents had taken down stenographically. But in none of his sermons did Pastor Niemoeller exhort his congregation to overthrow the Nazi regime. He merely raised his voice against some of the Nazi policies, particularly the policy directed against the Church. He had even refrained from criticizing the Nazi government itself or any of its personnel. Under the former government his sermons would have been construed only as an exercise of the right of free speech. Now, however, written laws, no matter how explicitly they were worded, were subjected to the interpretation of the judges.[13]

In a June 27, 1937 sermon, Niemoeller made it clear to those in attendance that he had a sacred duty to speak out on the evils of the Nazi regime no matter what the consequences: "We have no more thought of using our own powers to escape the arm of the authorities than had the Apostles of old. No more are we ready to keep silent at man's behest when God commands us to speak. For it is, and must remain, the case that we must obey God rather than man."[14] A few days later, he was arrested. His crime? "Abuse of the pulpit."

Shirer paints a depressing picture of the state of the Christian church in 1938. The "Special Courts" set up by the Nazis made claims against pastors who spoke out against Hitler's policies. Niemoeller was not the only one singled out by the Gestapo. "Some 807 other pastors and leading laymen of the 'Confessional Church' were arrested in 1937, and hundreds more in the next couple of years."[15] A group of Confessional Churches in Germany, founded by Pastor Niemoeller and other Protestant ministers, drew up a proclamation to confront the political changes taking place in Germany that threatened the people "with a deadly danger. The danger lies in a new religion," the proclamation declared. "The church has by order of its Master to see to it that in our people Christ is given the honor that is proper to the Judge of the world . . . The First Commandment says 'Thou shalt have no other gods before me.' The new religion is a rejection of the First Commandment."[16] Five hundred pastors who read the proclamation from their pulpits were arrested. "Not many Germans lost much sleep over the arrests of a few thousand pastors and priests."[17]

A recent discovery of a confidential U.S. government report that was prepared by the Office of Strategic Services, a forerunner of the CIA, for the International Military Tribunal at Nuremburg, Germany, documents how the Nazis wanted to "take over the churches from within, using party sympathizers." The usurpation of ecclesiastical authority would be accomplished by discrediting, jailing, or even killing Christian leaders and then re-indoctrinating the members of the congregations to "give them a new faith—in Germany's Third Reich." The ultimate goal was to "eliminate Christianity." The 120-page official document titled *The Nazi Master Plan: The Persecution of the Christian Churches* reported the following to the Military Tribunal in 1945:

> Important leaders of the National Socialist party would have liked to meet this situation [church influence] by complete extirpation [removal] of Christianity and the substitution of a purely racial religion. . . . The best evidence now available as to the existence of an anti-Church plan is to be found in the systematic nature of the persecution itself. . . . Different steps in that persecution, such as the campaign for the suppression of denominational and youth organizations, the campaign against denominational schools, the defamation campaign against the clergy, started on the same day in the whole area of the Reich. . . and were supported by the entire regimented press, by Nazi Party meetings, by traveling party speakers.[18]

Churches were "confined as far as possible to the performance of narrowly religious functions, and even within this narrow sphere were subjected to as many hindrances as the Nazis dared to impose. Implementation of this objective started with the curtailment of religious instruction in the primary and secondary schools with the squeezing of the religious periods into inconvenient hours, with Nazi propaganda among the teachers in order to induce them to refuse the teaching of religion, with vetoing of . . . religious text books, and finally with substituting Nazi *Weltanschauung* [world-and-life view] and 'German faith' for Christian religious denominational instruction. . . . At the time of the outbreak of the war . . . religious instruction had practically disappeared from Germany's primary schools." [19]

Hitler knew that to secure the future, he had to take hold of the present and reshape the worldview of a new generation with his Nazi-constructed worldview. By controlling the schools and churches and hijacking the educational process in both institutions, Hitler had eliminated competing transmission belts of ideological resistance.

Marxism

The Marxist worldview, as put forth by Lenin, had similar aspirations. Education had to be centralized. The State would become the educator, the new parent. While in a Christian context, schools act in a delegated capacity as *en loco parentis* ("in place of the parents"), under communism, the roles are reversed so that homes and schools reflect and perpetuate the agenda of the State. Like its future Nazi rival, the goal was to indoctrinate the youth with an alien worldview. Marxism's optimistic secular eschatology allowed for an ideological purge of remnants of the older Christian worldview from the newly established materialist State religion based on Darwinian principles. To speed up the process, systematic exterminations were the order of the day:

> A large percentage of the generation that knew Joseph Stalin died as a direct result of his directives. These were purely political killings, "exterminations," "liquidations" of "the enemy class" and "undesirable elements." How many were involved? Solzhenitsyn's estimates reach as high as sixty million. Robert Conquest, author of *The Great Terror*,[20] fixed the number at well into the millions. It is doubtful if we will ever know the true total—God alone knows.[21]

Like Hitler, Lenin saw the value in monopolizing education and bringing it under the exclusive control of the State. He believed that time was on his side. The old order would pass away along with its outdated ideas regarding religion, family, and education. The process for change, however, had to begin with the children. The sooner they could be taken from their parents and broken from their links to the past, the sooner the reprogramming could take place. In his *Principles of Communism,* published in 1847, Engels had advocated the "education of all children, as soon as they are old enough to dispense with maternal care, in national institutions and at the charge of the nation."[22] All facets of society must conform to the new ideology:

> We are bringing the women into the social economy, into legislation and government. . . . We are establishing communal kitchens . . . infant asylums . . . educational institutions of all kinds. In short, we are seriously carrying out the demand of our program for the transference of the economic and educational function of the separate household to society. . . . The children are brought up under more favourable conditions than at home. . . .[23]

Education was centralized. The "separate household" was transferred "to society." Mothers would be encouraged to enter the work force in ever greater numbers. This would allow the State an opportunity to care for the children in "educational institutions of all kinds."

The Long March Through the Institutions

The oppressive nature of the older Communism was noted by Antonio Gramsci (1891–1937), a committed Marxist with a new approach to bring about cultural and social change. In order to capture democratic nations, a new model would have to be developed. Like the revolutionary Marxists before him, Gramsci considered Christianity to be the "force binding all the classes—peasants and workers and princes, priests and popes and all the rest besides, into a single, homogeneous culture. It was specifically Christian culture, in which individual men and women understood that the most important things about human life transcend the material conditions in which they lived out their mortal lives."[24]

Gramsci broke with Marx and Lenin's belief that the masses would rise up and overthrow the ruling "superstructure." No matter how oppressed the working classes might be, their Christian faith would not allow such an overthrow, Gramsci theorized. Marxism taught "that everything valuable in life was within mankind,"[25] but this unbridled secularism was rejected by Christians. Perceptively, Gramsci realized that in the long run what people did not ultimately believe in they would not fight for. Was Gramsci right? "The only Marxist state that existed" in Gramsci's day "was imposed and maintained by force and by terrorist policies that duplicated and even exceeded the worst facets of Mussolini's Fascism."[26] The building of the Berlin Wall was the most visible evidence of Gramsci's early critique of traditional Marxism. Walls had to be built to keep people from escaping the "Workers' Paradise."

While Gramsci was still a committed Marxist and "totally convinced that the material dimension of everything in the universe, including mankind, was the whole of it,"[27] he believed that the road taken to "utopia" by traditional Marxists was one lined with formidable obstacles. Gramsci began his re-imaging of Marxism by dropping the harsh slogans. "It wouldn't do to rant about 'revolution' and 'dictatorship of the proletariat' and the 'Workers' Paradise.'"[28] Instead, Marxism would have to put on a new face and talk about "national consensus," "national unity," and "national pacification." The democratic process rather than revolution would be used to bring about the necessary changes. At first, pluralism would be promoted and defended. Further, Marxists would join with other oppressed groups—even if they did not share Marxist ideals—to create a unified coalition of voting power. After building their coalition "they must enter into every civil, cultural and political activity in every nation, patiently leavening them all as thoroughly as yeast leavens bread."[29] To change the culture, Gramsci argued, "would require a 'long march through the institutions'—the arts, cinema, theater, schools, colleges, seminaries, newspapers, magazines, and the new electronic medium [of the time], radio."[30]

Following Gramsci's paradigm, the mind had to be stripped of any notion of the transcendent—"that there is nothing beyond the matter of this universe. There is nothing in existence that transcends man—his material organism within his material surroundings."[31] The pagan notion of the separation of the two realms (spiritual/material, heaven/earth)[32] that has dogged orthodox Christianity since the first century had to be reintroduced and reinforced:

> In the most practical terms, he needed to get individuals and groups in every class and station of life to think about life's problems without reference to the Christian transcendent, without reference to God and the laws of God. He needed to get them to react with antipathy and positive opposition to any introduction of Christian ideals or the Christian transcendent into the treatment and solution of the problems of modern life.[33]

The here and now must be absolutized and made the reference point for everything we think and do. "Everything must be done in the name of man's dignity and rights, and in the name of his autonomy and freedom from outside constraint. From the claims and constraints of Christianity, above all."[34] Has Gramsci been successful? You be the judge:

- What a person does in his private life does not affect his ability to govern.
- It's just about sex, even if it's adultery.
- Religion and politics don't mix.
- You can't impose your morality on others.
- You can't legislate morality.
- Religion has no business in the classroom; it's a private affair.
- There's a separation between Church (God) and State.

The transcendent is no longer a viable reference point in American public schools. All of life is immanent, that is, all that counts is this world. America is haunted by the ghost of Antonio Gramsci, and the specter of his image roams the halls of every public school in America.

The Secularists

The above examples from Nazism and Communism might seem like extreme examples of educational tyranny, but modern-day "Brights,"[35] as they like to call themselves, have some equally startling things to say about education. Daniel C. Dennett, a high priest of the evolutionary dogma, encapsulates the character of a self-professed secular[36] worldview:

> If you insist on teaching your children falsehoods—that the Earth is flat,[37] that "Man" is not a product of evolution by natural selection—then you must expect, at the very least, that those of us who have freedom of speech will feel free to describe your teachings as the spreading of falsehoods, and will attempt to demonstrate this to your children at our earliest opportunity. Our future well-being—the well-being of all of us on the planet—depends on the education of our descendants."[38]

Coercion is the name of the game. If Dennett had his way, parents could not make educational choices for their children. The Nazis had their "Hitler Youth," and this evolutionist wants to have his "Darwin Youth." Educational coercion is not a relic of the past. In Germany today, Christian parents are denied the right to educate their children at home.[39]

The modern-day public school has adopted the opening line of Carl Sagan's *Cosmos* as its operating assumption for learning: "The cosmos is all that is or ever was or ever will be."[40] Every fact, experience, and piece of scientific evidence that is gathered must be filtered through this man-made, indefensible, and improvable interpretive grid. All that follows in the *Cosmos* worldview is measured by this one-sentence interpretive yardstick rather than "according to Christ" (Col. 2:8) who "made the world" and "upholds all things by the word of His power" (Heb. 1:2, 3). Where the Bible presupposes God and His creative activity (Gen. 1:1; Heb. 11:3), Sagan presupposes the cosmos and nothing else.

For Sagan, the cosmos was god, a glorious accidental substitute for what he believed were ancient, pre-scientific beliefs about God and the origin and nature of the universe. The very idea of a *personal* God is, in Sagan's worldview, simply "the dreams of men."[41] Even so, Sagan's worldview is just as religious as that of the Christian's worldview:

> When Sagan excludes even the possibility that a spiritual dimension has any place in his cosmos—not even at the unknown, mysterious moment when life began—he makes accidental evolution the explanation for everything. Presented in this way, evolution does indeed look like an inverted religion, a conceptual golden calf, which manages to reek of sterile atheism. It is little wonder that many parents find their deeper emotions stirred if they discover this to be the import of Johnny's education.[42]

Sagan worshiped an eternal cosmos that he *presupposed* is an evolutionary substitute for the eternal God of the Bible who gives life and meaning to everything. Sagan said it like this: "It is the universe that made us. . . . We are creatures of the cosmos. . . . Our obligation to survive and flourish is owed, not just to ourselves, but also to that cosmos, ancient and vast, from which we spring."[43] God's personal attributes are imputed to an impersonal cosmos. The "primordial biotic soup"[44] nourished our ancient ancestors as they emerged from that first ocean of life. These memories, according to Sagan, are eternally etched on our evolved psyche.

The ocean calls. Some part of our being knows this is from where we came. We long to return. These aspirations are not, I think, irreverent, although they may trouble whatever gods may be.[45]

Sagan makes it clear that there are no "gods" in the usual sense in his universe, only "accidents"[46] that somehow developed into designed and meaningful entities. At times, however, Sagan muses rhapsodic over a seemingly benign reverence of the cosmos that hints at a deep religious commitment to atheism and elements of paganism. "Our ancestors worshipped the sun," he reflects, "and they were far from foolish. It makes good sense to revere the sun and the stars, because we are their children."[47] But who made the cosmos? How did the cosmos get here? Why are there order and complexity in the cosmos? Sagan never answered these questions. He could not as long as the cosmos is all that is ever was or ever will be.

So then, the Christian, the pagan, and the atheist interpret the world by an appeal to a set of essential materialistic, this-world-only presuppositions that cannot account for non-material entities like reason, logic, love, compassion, good, and evil. All worldviews—even those espousing atheism—are presuppositionally religious. "This means that many people may rightly call themselves atheists meaning that they do not believe there are any gods ('a-theist' means literally 'no-god'), but they will still have a religious belief if they regard anything whatever as the self-existent on which all else depends."[48] Those beliefs "on which all else depends" are presuppositions, and everyone has them, from the bushman and the astronomer to the philosopher and the classroom teacher. While many teachers might not believe this radicalized secular worldview, they are increasingly obligated to teach it.

Notes

1. Herbert Schlossberg, *Idols for Destruction: Christian Faith and Its Confrontation with American Society* (Wheaton, IL: Crossway Books, [1983] 1993), 209.

2. William L. Shirer, *The Rise and Fall of the Third Reich* (New York: Simon and Schuster, 1960), 248–249.

3. Shirer, *Rise and Fall of the Third Reich*, 249.

4. Shirer, *Rise and Fall of the Third Reich*, 249.

5. Shirer, *Rise and Fall of the Third Reich*, 249.

6. C. Gregg Singer, *From Rationalism to Irrationality: The Decline of the Western Mind from the Renaissance to the Present* (Phillipsburg, NJ: Presbyterian and Reformed, 1979), 28.

7. Randy Thomasson, president of the Campaign for Children and Families, explains, "It's because Christian colleges and churches have ignored the political process for so long. Now the political process, absent religious values, is coming back to assault the church." ("Gov. Arnold tosses school moral codes" [August 29, 2006]: www.worldnetdaily.com/news/article.asp?ARTICLE_ID=51732).

8. Shirer, *The Rise and Fall of the Third Reich*, 240.

9. Shirer, *The Rise and Fall of the Third Reich*, 240.

10. William Shirer, *The Nightmare Years: 1930–1940* (Boston, MA: Little, Brown and Company, 1984), 156.

11. Donald D. Wall, "The Lutheran Response to the Hitler Regime in Germany," ed. Robert D. Linder, *God and Caesar: Case Studies in the Relationship Between Christianity and the State* (Longview, TX: The Conference on Faith and History, 1971), 88.

12. Basil Miller, *Martin Niemoeller: Hero of the Concentration Camp*, 5th ed. (Grand Rapids, MI: Zondervan, 1942), 112.

13. Leo Stein, *I Was in Hell with Niemoeller* (New York: Fleming H. Revell, 1942), 175.

14. Quoted in Shirer, *The Rise and Fall of the Third Reich*, 239.

15. Shirer, *The Rise and Fall of the Third Reich*, 239.

16. Quoted in Eugene Davidson, *The Trials of the Germans: An Account of the Twenty-Two Defendants before the International Military Tribunal at Nuremberg* (Columbia, MO: University of Missouri Press, [1966] 1997), 275.

17. Shirer, *The Rise and Fall of the Third Reich*, 240.

18. Quoted in Edward Colimore, "Papers reveal Nazi aim: End Christianity," *Philadelphia Inquirer* (January 9, 2002). http://inq.philly.com/content/inquirer/2002/01/09/front_page/JNAZI09.htm

19. The report is available online at www.camlaw.rutgers.edu/publications/law-religion/nuremberg/nurinst1.htm

20. Robert Conquest has a done a major revision of *The Great Terror* using newly available evidence from the *glasnost* era: *The Great Terror: A Reassessment* (New York: Oxford University Press, 1990). Also see Mark Kramer, ed., *The Black Book of Communism: Crimes, Terror, Repression* (Cambridge, MA: Harvard University Press, 1999).

21. Lloyd Billingsley, *The Generation that Knew Not Josef* (Portland, OR: Multnomah Press, 1985), 37. During the era of *glasnost*, Stalin's past had literally been dug up. "A government commission has found that thousands of skulls and bones buried in a mass grave outside Kiev were those of victims killed during dictator Josef Stalin's repressions, not by Nazi soldiers, Tass, the state-run news agency, has reported." ("Mass Grave Near Kiev Holds Stalin's Victims, Panel Says," *St. Louis Post-Dispatch* [March 26, 1989]). Under Stalin, "more than 600,000 death sentences" were meted

out and "at least five million" people were arrested "in the worst years of 1937–38. He destroyed children as well as old people, nobodies and party favorites. . . . In the countryside in 1932–33, as many as eight million starved to death in accordance with an agricultural policy based on killing *kulaks* (farmers) outright or just wasting their lands." (Peter Keresztes, "Murder of Millions," *The Wall Street Journal* [August 31, 1989], A13).

22. Quoted in Francis Nigel Lee, *Communist Eschatology: A Christian Philosophical Analysis of the Post-Capitalistic Views of Marx, Engels and Lenin* (Nutley, NJ: The Craig Press, 1974), 351.

23. Quoted in Lee, *Communist Eschatology*, 350.

24. Malachi Martin, *The Keys of This Blood: The Struggle for World Dominion Between Pope John II, Mikhail Gorbachev and the Capitalist West* (New York: Simon and Schuster, 1990), 245.

25. Martin, *The Keys of This Blood*, 245.

26. Martin, *The Keys of This Blood*, 248.

27. Martin, *The Keys of This Blood*, 248.

28. Martin, *The Keys of This Blood*, 249.

29. Martin, *The Keys of This Blood*, 250.

30. Patrick J. Buchanan, *Death of the West: How Dying Populations and Immigrant Invasions Imperil Our Country and Civilization* (New York: St. Martin's Press/Thomas Dunne Books, 2001), 77.

31. Martin, *The Keys of This Blood*, 251.

32. See Peter E. Gillquist, *Why We Haven't Changed the World* (Fleming H. Revell, 1982), 43.

33. Martin, *The Keys of This Blood*, 251.

34. Martin, *The Keys of This Blood*, 251.

35. See Gary DeMar, "A Bright Responds" (August 16, 2006): http://americanvision.org/articlearchive/08-16-06.asp. Also see Regis Nicoll, "Putting on a 'Bright' face" (August 11, 2006): http://www.americanvision.org/articlearchive/08-11-06.asp

36. The adjective secular comes from the Latin *saeculum*, which means "time" or "age." "To call someone secular means he is completely time-bound, totally a child of his age, a creature of history, with no vision of eternity. Unable to see anything in the perspective of eternity, he cannot believe God exists or acts in human affairs." (James Hitchcock, *What is Secular Humanism?* [Ann Arbor, MI: Servant Publications, 1982], 10–11). A secularist denies special revelation, not only the "absurdity" of God addressing man but the impossibility of it.

37. On the "flat-earth myth," see Gary DeMar, *America's Christian History: The Untold Story* (Powder Springs, GA: American Vision, 1995), 221–234; Gary DeMar and Fred Douglas Young, *To Pledge Allegiance: A New World in View* (Atlanta, GA: American Vision, 1996), 75–82; Jeffrey Burton Russell, *Inventing the Flat Earth: Columbus and Modern Historians* (New York: Praeger, 1991). This topic will be covered in more detail in Chapter 14.

38. Daniel C. Dennett, *Darwin's Dangerous Idea: Evolution and the Meaning of Life* (New York: Simon and Schuster, 1995), 519.

39. "'Homeschooling Illegal' Declares German School Official" (January 7, 2005): www.hslda.org/hs/international/Germany/200501100.asp

40. Carl Sagan, *Cosmos* (New York: Random House, 1980), 4.

41. Sagan, *Cosmos*, 257.

42. William R. Fix, *The Bone Peddlers: Selling Evolution* (New York: Macmillan Publishing Co., 1984), xxiv.

43. From the 13-hour television presentation of *Cosmos* aired in the fall of 1980. Quoted in Richard A. Baer, Jr., "They *Are* Teaching Religion in the Public Schools," *Christianity Today* (February 17, 1984), 12.

44. Prebiotic means "before life." It refers to the hypothesis put forth by the Russian scientist A.I. Oparin who claimed that life began in a sea of chemicals called a *prebiotic soup*. The chance occurrence of chemicals and compounds eventually led to molecules. The theory does not explain where the chemicals and compounds came from and how they organized themselves into complex life.

45. Sagan, *Cosmos*, 5.

46. Sagan, *Cosmos*, 30.

47. Quoted in Baer, "They *Are* Teaching Religion in the Public Schools," 13.

48. Roy A. Clouser, *The Myth of Religious Neutrality: An Essay on the Hidden Role of Religious Belief in Theories* (Notre Dame, IN: University of Notre Dame Press, 1991), 26–27.

Schools at Risk

There can be, therefore, no true education without moral culture,
and no true moral culture without Christianity. The very power of
the teacher in the school-room is either moral or it is a degrading
force. But he can show the child no other moral basis for it than the
Bible. Hence my argument is as perfect as clear. The teacher must
be Christian. But the American Commonwealth has promised to
have no religious character. Then it cannot be [our] teacher.[1]

F OR THE MOST part, education is centralized and controlled by civil
government at both the state and national levels. Women are entering the work force for various reasons, mostly out of financial necessity. Our nation's tax structure is a burden on families. The continuing rise in the Social Security tax is financially handicapping the family. State governments are pushing for a longer school year and earlier attendance requirements (e.g., compulsory kindergarten). Today's educational establishment is in academic and moral crisis. The April 1983 publication *A Nation at Risk* "expressed alarm at the marked deterioration of academic study in our secondary schools."

> Secondary school curricula have been homogenized, diluted, and
> diffused to the point that they no longer have a central purpose.

In effect, we have a cafeteria-style curriculum in which the appe-
tizers and desserts can easily be mistaken for the main courses.[2]

Since the publication of the *A Nation at Risk Study*, government controlled education has gotten progressively worse, and yet most Christian parents are either unaware of the crisis or are indifferent to it.[3] In
addition, there is a moral crisis. "A generation ago, American public
schools began to walk away from their role as moral educators. Schools
feared they would be accused of imposing religion or 'indoctrinating'
children, so they stuck to academics, leaving moral instruction to parents and the community."[4] In time, moral education returned in the
form of indoctrination.

No Moral Cure

In light of all of this, a number of frustrated parent groups, conservative
organizations, and educators are calling for a new approach to moral
education. One school district in Maryland has chosen to teach 24 core
values from the Constitution.[5] But why are these values "core values"?
On what ethical standard does the Constitution rest? The Constitution
itself does not say, unless it's "We the people." But by basing morality
on what a majority of people say only takes the discussion back a step.
Democracy, from the Greek word *demos* (people), is no moral cure-all
since it's the people who are in need of an education that is not a form
of indoctrination by the State.

John Winthrop (1588–1649), first governor of Massachusetts Bay
Colony, declared *direct* democracy to be "the meanest and worst of all
forms of government."[6] John Cotton (1584–1652), seventeenth-century
minister from Massachusetts, in 1636 wrote the following about the inherent dangers found in a political system based on pure democracy:
"Democracy, I do not conceive that ever God did ordain as a fit government either for church or commonwealth. If the people be governors,
who shall be governed?"[7] Lest you think that these are extreme views of
religious kill-joys, consider the opinion of our nation's constitutional-
founders. James Madison (1751–1836), recognized as the "father of the

Constitution," wrote that democracies are "spectacles of turbulence and contention." Pure democracies are "incompatible with personal security or the rights of property. . . . In general [they] have been as short in their lives as they have been violent in their deaths."[8] John Adams, the second president of the United States, stated that "the voice of the people is 'sometimes the voice of Mahomet, of Caesar, of Catiline, the Pope, and the Devil.'"[9] Francis A. Schaeffer described democracy as "the dictatorship of the 51%, with no controls and nothing with which to challenge the majority."[10] The logic is simple: "It means that if Hitler was able to get a 51% vote of the Germans, he had a right to kill the Jews."[11]

An Appeal to International Law

Unfortunately, there is no consensus on morality except when consensus opinion works to promote the goals of the State. A number of universities are designing a curriculum that will include a number of non-western texts that will have the effect of diluting the impact the Bible has had on our legal system. This will mean a shift in values from a once-unified Western (Christian) ethical system to a smorgasbord (pluralistic) cultural ethical system defined by the State. The courts are following a similar pattern, but they are picking only those international laws that already support their views. The judges go "nation shopping" to find legal decisions that agree with their pre-determined opinions on ethical matters. They then claim that international law is on their side on issues such as abortion and homosexuality. Consider these comments by Supreme Court Justice Antonin Scalia:

> According to the United Nations, the United States is now one of only fifty-three countries classified as allowing abortion on demand, versus one hundred and thirty-nine countries allowing it only under particular circumstances, or not at all. Among those countries the UN classified—this is in 2001—as not allowing abortion on demand were the United Kingdom, Finland, Iceland, India, Ireland, Japan, Luxemburg, Mexico, New Zealand, Portugal, Spain, Switzerland and virtually all of South America. Yet the court has generally ignored foreign law in its abortion cases. [*Planned*

Parenthood v. Casey, 505 U.S. 833 (1992)] does not mention it all;
[*Roe v. Wade*, 410 U.S. 113 (1973)] discusses only modern British
law—which, in any event, is more restrictive than what Roe held.
I will become a believer in the ingenuousness—though never in
the propriety—of the Court's newfound respect for the wisdom of
foreign minds when it applies that wisdom in the abortion cases.[12]

In 1991, Georgia rejected the high school textbook *Triumph of the American Nation*, "criticizing its 'outdated approach, inattention to multiculturalism, inadequate critical thinking questions, and choppy narrative flow.' . . . The new Todd and Curti [textbook] exemplifies disturbing trends in social studies publishing today. It is a big step backward, a case of 'dumbing down' and revisionist folly in search of a larger audience. No 'Triumph' remains in the title, except for the many forces in contemporary culture that seek to transform the curriculum along the fault lines of multiculturalism."[13]

A standard of right and wrong outside individuals and the State must be found—a standard that is greater than man or the State. *Vox populi, vox dei*, "The voice of the people is the voice of God" is no better remedy than the voice of the Department of Education is the voice of God. Only the Triune God of Scripture can set forth what is right or wrong. But this cannot work in today's educational atmosphere. Such an approach would mean "indoctrinating" students. Let's face facts. Children are indoctrinated the first day they enter a classroom. All teachers espouse a moral code. Increasingly, that moral code comes as a directive by the State that teachers must incorporate into their teaching. If a teacher can't say something is right or wrong unless the State sanctions it, then anything goes and usually does.

For example, sex education, as it was originally conceived, was to teach the basics of how the reproduction system worked as part of basic biology instruction. There was no attempt to use such instruction as a how-to manual for sexual practice. Biological, anatomical, and physiological teaching was done within a moral context because the school was seen as an extension of the home. This is no longer the case. School systems are beginning to use biology classes as a way to indoctrinate children to accept so-called alternative lifestyles that include the claim that homosexual behavior is normal sexual behavior.

The Virtuecrats

Well intentioned attempts have been made to fix the problem. William Bennett, who has been described as the nation's leading "virtuecrat,"[14] has been calling "for a new approach to moral education, one that gives kids a grounding in … 'those values all Americans share.'"[15]

> Bennett, though frank and provocative, has a keen sense of marketing and showmanship. While he upholds the value of religious faith, he distinguishes himself from TV evangelists and reaches a larger audience by keeping his discussion of virtues accessible even to secular readers and listeners.[16]

But Bennett is writing against the worn out backdrop of an older worldview where most people understood there was an agreed upon idea of what was right and wrong behavior based on some transcendental value system. At the same time, it was the belief of nearly all parents that they had some say in what their children were being taught. In this bygone era, parents and teachers agreed that the school was the extension of the home and a common value system. If there is still a consensus morality, one has to ask where this consensus originates. Bennett is a prime example of not defining the true origin of virtue for fear of it being excluded from the public school classroom because it will be considered "religious" and a violation of the "separation of church and state."

There was a time when there was less moral ambiguity. The early educational curriculum in American schools acknowledged that God's law was the foundation for morality. Even non-Christians have noted this: "As [Ted] Koppel observed, they are the Ten Commandments, not the Ten Suggestions. God's standards still apply against murder, stealing, lying, adultery, coveting the possessions of others, and homosexuality."[17] Ralph Reed, writing in his book *Active Faith*, observes:

The Christian view of homosexual practices derives from a belief in the moral principles of human sexuality found in the Bible. From descriptions in the Book of Genesis of the destruction of Sodom and Gomorrah and the injunctions against sexual misconduct in Leviticus to the apostle Paul's letter to the Romans, in both the Old and the New Testament, the Bible makes it clear that homosexuality is a deviation from normative sexual conduct and God's laws . . . . [T]he totality of Scripture is clear in treating homosexuality in the same terms as adultery, incest, and other forms of sexual temptation that deviate from God's plan of heterosexual conduct within the institution of a monogamous marriage.[18]

Don't get me wrong. Virtue is a good thing. Morality, even if it doesn't have a discernible foundation, is not all bad. Over time, however, "virtue" and "morality" can be made to mean anything. Homosexuals, for example, want to get in on the family-values bandwagon. They are adopting children and pursuing legislation that will make homosexual marriages legal and on an equal par with the biblical definition of marriage—one man married to one woman. Welcome to the world of family values homosexual style.

Modern educational theory lacks a comprehensive and cohesive worldview. The lack of a "central purpose" is at the heart of the problem. Only the Christian school—homeschool, private academy, or church-run—can fill the gap left by humanistic educational theories and programs.

Notes

1. Robert L. Dabney, *Discussions*, 4 vols. (Harrisonburg, VA: Sprinkle Publications, [1897] 1979), 4:222–223.

2. Quoted in William J. Bennett, *James Madison High School: A Curriculum for American Students* (Washington, D.C.: United States Department of Education, 1987), 1.

3. Bruce N. Shortt, *The Harsh Truth About Public Schools* (Vallecito, CA: Chalcedon Foundation, 2004).

4. Eleanor Smith, "The New Moral Classroom," *Psychology Today* (May 1989), 32. See William Kilpatrick, *Why Johnny Can't Tell Right from Wrong: Moral Illiteracy and the Case for Character Education* (New York: Simon & Schuster, 1992).

5. Smith, "The New Moral Classroom," 34.

6. Quoted in A. Marvyn Davies, *Foundation of American Freedom: Calvinism in the Development of Democratic Thought and Action* (Nashville, TN: Abingdon Press, 1955), 11.

7. Letter to Lord Say and Seal, quoted by Perry Miller and Thomas H. Johnson, eds., *The Puritans: A Sourcebook of Their Writings*, 2 vols. (New York: Harper and Row, [1938] 1963), 1:209–210. Also see Edwin Powers, *Crime and Punishment in Early Massachusetts: 1620–1692* (Boston, MA: Beacon Press, 1966), 55.

8. Quoted in Jacob E. Cooke, ed., *The Federalist*, (Middletown, CT: Wesleyan University Press, 1961), 61.

9. John Adams, quoted by Gilbert Chinard, *Honest John Adams* (Boston, MA: Little, Brown and Co., [1933] 1961), 241 in John Eidsmoe, "The Christian America Response to National Confessionalism," in Gary Scott Smith, ed., *God and Politics: Four Views on the Reformation of Civil Government* (Phillipsburg, NJ: Presbyterian and Reformed, 1989), 227–228.

10. Francis A. Schaeffer, *The Church at the End of the Twentieth Century* (1970) in *The Complete Works of Francis A. Schaeffer: A Christian Worldview*, 5 vols. (Westchester, IL: Crossway Books, 1982), 4:27.

11. Schaeffer, *The Church at the End of the Twentieth Century*, 4:27.

12. Antonin Scalia, "International Law in American Courts," The American Enterprise Institute (February 21, 2006): www.joink.com/homes/users/ninoville/aei2-21-06.asp.

13. Gilbert T. Sewall, "The Triumph of Textbook Trendiness," *Wall Street Journal* (March 1, 1994), A14.

14. Howard Fineman, "The Virtuecrats," *Newsweek* (June 13, 1994), 33.

15. *The Atlanta Journal and Constitution* (November 28, 1986), 49A.

16. Dan Goodgame, "The Chairman of Virtue Inc.," *Time* (September 16, 1996), 46–49.

17. Ralph Reed, *Active Faith: How Christians are Changing the Soul of American Politics* (New York: Free Press, 1996), 263.

18. Reed, *Active Faith*, 264–265.

A Good Beginning Gone Bad

From the very beginnings, the expressed purpose of colonial education had been to preserve society against barbarism, and, so far as possible, against sin. The inculcation of a saving truth was primarily the responsibility of the churches, but schools were necessary to protect the written means of revelation.[1]

THE REFORMATION OF the sixteenth century stressed the reclamation of all of life, with education as an essential focal point. Samuel Blumenfeld, author of *Is Public Education Necessary?* and *The Victims of Dick and Jane*, writes:

> Since the Protestant rebellion against Rome had arisen in part as a result of Biblical study and interpretation, it became obvious to Protestant leaders that if the Reform movement were to survive and flourish, widespread Biblical literacy, at all levels of society, would be absolutely necessary. The Bible was to be the moral and spiritual authority in every man's life, and therefore an intimate knowledge of it was imperative if a new Protestant social order were to take root.[2]

Martin Luther in Germany (1483–1546) and John Calvin (1509–1564) in Geneva, Switzerland, established schools to meet the needs of those who saw the Bible as God's Word that applied to every area of life. The outgrowth of the gospel included the redemption of all of life, not just the salvation of the soul. In fact, Calvin's Academy in Geneva, founded by John Calvin in 1559, attracted students from all over Europe. Charles Borgeaud, a historian on the Academy, wrote that "Calvin had achieved his task: he had secured the future of Geneva . . . making it at once a church, a school and a fortress. It was the first stronghold of liberty in modern times." The effects of the training at Geneva were far reaching: "It was not only the future of Geneva but that of other regions as well that was affected by the rise of the Geneva schools. The men who were to lead the advance of the Reformed Church in many lands were trained in Geneva classrooms, preached Geneva doctrines, and sang the Psalms to Geneva tunes."[3]

A New World Education

In our own nation one of the first acts performed in the New World was the establishment of schools. The Puritan system was a copy of Geneva.[4] The purpose of these colonial schools was to further the gospel of Christ in all disciplines.

> Regardless of the vocation for which a student was preparing, the colonial college sought to provide for him an education that was distinctly Christian. At Harvard the original goal of higher learning was "to know God and Jesus Christ which is eternal life (John 17:3), and therefore to lay Christ in the bottom as the only foundation of all sound knowledge and learning." Yale in the early 1700s stated as its primary goal that "every student shall consider the main end of his study to wit to know God in Jesus Christ and answerably to lead a Godly, sober life."[5]

The same theme was echoed over 100 years later at the founding of King's College in New York, the predecessor of Columbia University. An advertisement appeared in the *New York Mercury* on June 3, 1754, announcing the opening of King's College. The advertisement had been placed by Samuel Johnson (1696–1772), a graduate of Yale. Similar to the guidelines demanded by Harvard and Yale, King's College required knowledge of Latin and Greek. Although the college was affiliated with the Anglican Church, the advertisement assured students that "there is no intention to impose on the scholars the peculiar tenets of any particular sect of Christians, but to inculcate upon their tender minds the great principles of Christianity and morality in which true Christians of each denomination are generally agreed."[6] The advertisement went on to state:

> The chief thing that is aimed at in this college is to teach and engage the children to know God in Jesus Christ and to love and serve Him in all sobriety, godliness, and righteousness of life, with perfect heart and a willing mind, and to train them up in all virtuous habits and all such useful knowledge as may render them creditable to their families and friends, ornaments to their country, and useful to the public weal in their generations.[7]

The original shield of King's College was adopted in 1755. The college's commitment to a biblical worldview is evident in the shield's figures and inscriptions. Over the head of the seated woman is the (Hebrew) Tetragrammaton, YHVH (*Jehovah*); the Latin motto around her head means "In Thy light we see light" (Psalm 36:10); the Hebrew phrase on the ribbon is *Uri El* ("God is my light"), an allusion to Psalm 27:1; and at the feet of the woman is the New Testament passage commanding Christians to desire the pure milk of God's word (1 Peter 2:1–2).[8] Columbia long ago adopted a new seal. The only line remaining from the original is the Latin phrase "In Thy light we see light" without any reference to its biblical source.[9]

The Puritan educational system trained church and civil leaders. The emphasis, however, was to prepare men intellectually so that future generations would not be left with "an illiterate ministry" since the pulpit was the means by which the colonies received their news and instruction. The training that went on in these earliest colonial schools affected the entire colony. The minister became the spiritual leader as well as the town's news reporter, political pundit, and futurist.

> Unlike modern mass media, the sermon stood alone in local New England contexts as the only regular (at least weekly) medium of public communication. As a channel of information, it combined religious, educational, and journalistic functions, and supplied all the key terms necessary to understand existence in this world and the next. As the only event in public assembly that regularly brought the entire community together, it also represented the central ritual of social order and control.[10]

Many of these preachers became instructors in the early colleges. "Although each of the three earliest colleges, Harvard, William and Mary, and Yale, was chartered by the established church in its colony, each also held a direct relationship to the state and served as the center for training civic as well as clerical leaders for its region."[11] For example, James Madison, considered to be the architect and "Father of the Constitution," studied under Rev. John Witherspoon at the College of New Jersey, a Presbyterian college now known as Princeton. At Princeton, even those who did not enter the gospel ministry, were expected to know their "Bible from cover to cover." The curriculum of Harvard, for example, emphasized the study of biblical languages, logic, divinity (theology), and skills in communication (public speaking and rhetoric). Churches expected their ministers to read the Scriptures in the original languages.

Since civil government was a major concern in the colonies, courses in ethics, politics, and history were also required. Many of the constitutional framers of the eighteenth century were steeped in basic Bible doctrines. These biblical concepts found their way into our political system (e.g., decentralized political power, checks and balances, a republican form of government, abhorrence of an absolute democracy, jurisdictional separation between Church and State, the protection of private property, the gold standard, keeping of the Lord's Day, protection of Christian worship, etc.). These principles are most evident in the state constitutions and the Articles of Confederation.

Courses in law and medicine were also offered along with instruction in astronomy, physics, botany, science, and mathematics. Kirk House writes that Cotton Mather, who was born in 1663, graduated from "Harvard at age 18 and joined his father in his Boston pastorate. . . . Widely regarded as the most brilliant man in New England, he wrote 450 books and was a Fellow of the Royal Society." In addition to his theological studies, Mather was a scientist who "successfully introduced smallpox inoculation during the 1721 epidemic, and had his house bombed for his trouble."[12] It's not hard to understand how people might oppose inoculations, for both religious and scientific reasons, since healthy people were deliberately exposed to a life-threatening disease that had killed six people.

A Paradigm Shift

The churches expected their ministers "to be broadly learned, and, since the ancient classics were valued as timeless sources of wisdom and truth, it was important to have a sophisticated knowledge of Latin and Greek language and literature."[13] A leading historian of American education, Samuel Eliot Morrison, has shown that there were three elements in Harvard's curriculum. First, there were the seven liberal arts of the medieval university, as well as the study of the "Three Philosophies," law, medicine, and theology. Second, the student studied the literature of the classical world of Greek and Roman thought. Finally, the student had to learn the three "learned languages," Latin, Greek, and Hebrew. Morrison adds that "the last two elements had entered university curricula at the Renaissance."[14] This enabled them to read the Bible in the original languages, while Latin made classical works available for study as well.

If we follow modern histories of education in the time leading up to and following the Reformation, science took a back seat to progress. The main line of argument is that the study of science was antithetical to the study of the Bible. Of course, this is contrary to the facts of history. Most of the finest scientists of the era were devout Christians, and those that did not profess any particular religious affiliation still operated within the context of a Christian worldview where the world made sense because it was believed to be created by God.[15] The world was rational because God was rational.

In cultures where progress was made in mathematics, science, medicine, political theory, and law, people assumed that the world was not an illusion, that truth mattered, and man was a rational being created by a rational God even though at times man behaved irrationally and believed irrational things. Cultures that believed that spirits inhabited trees, rocks, and animals made very little progress culturally and scientifically because they never knew what the spirits might do. There was never a guarantee that what people did one day could be repeated on another day. They were at the mercy of what they believed were impersonal forces controlled by capricious gods who were always changing the rules.

> Pagan religions are typically animistic or pantheistic, treating the natural world either as the abode of the divine or as an emanation of God's own essence. The most familiar form of animism holds that spirits or gods reside in nature. In the words of Harvey Cox, a Baptist theologian, pagan man "lives in an enchanted forest." Glens and groves, rocks and streams are alive with spirits, sprites, demons. Nature teems with sun gods, river goddesses, astral deities.[16]

These false operational assumptions meant that the world could not be studied in a reliable and systematic way. "As long as nature commands religious worship, dissecting her is judged impious. As long as the world is charged with divine beings and powers, the only appropriate response is to supplicate them or ward them off."[17] As a result, technological, medical, scientific, and moral progress came to a standstill in cultures where people could not agree on basic operating assumptions of how and why things work the way they do. Biblical presuppositions about how the world worked changed the way the cosmos was studied.

Notes

1. Henry F. May, *The Enlightenment in America* (New York: Oxford University Press, 1976), 32–33.

2. Samuel L. Blumenfeld, *Is Public Education Necessary?* (Greenwich, CT: Devin-Adair, 1981), 10.

3. John T. McNeill, *The History and Character of Calvinism* (New York: Oxford University Press, 1954), 196.

4. David W. Hall, *The Genevan Reformation and the American Founding* (Lanham, MD: Lexington Books, 2003).

5. William C. Ringenberg, *The Christian College: A History of Protestant Higher Education in America*, 2nd ed. (Grand Rapids, MI: Baker, [1984] 2006), 38.

6. "Advertisement on the Opening of Kings College," in Sol Cohen, ed., *Education in the United States: A Documentary History*, 5 vols. (New York: Random House, 1974), 2:675.

7. "Advertisement on the Opening of Kings College," in Cohen, *Education in the United States*, 2:675.

8. The image is reproduced in Gabriel Sivan, *The Bible and Civilization* (New York: Quadrangle/New York Times Book Co., 1973), 237 and online at www.cheme.columbia.edu/img_base/r12c23b_123x124_shield.gif

9. www.cisl.columbia.edu/grads/tuku/research/figures/ColumbiaShield.jpg

10. Harry S. Stout, *The New England Soul: Preaching and Religious Culture in Colonial New England* (New York: Oxford University Press, 1986), 3.

11. Ringenberg, *The Christian College*, 42.

12. Kirk House, *God's Claims on Your Children: Readings in the Last 2000 Years of Christian Education* (Sterling, VA: GAM Printers, 1977), 61.

13. Ringenberg, *Christian College*, 46.

14. Samuel Eliot Morrison, *The Founding of Harvard College* (Cambridge, MA: Harvard University Press, 1935), 29.

15. Rodney Stark, *For the Glory of God* (Princeton, NJ: Princeton University Press, 2003), 198–199.

16. Nancy R. Pearcey and Charles B. Thaxton, *The Soul of Science: Christian Faith and Natural Philosophy* (Wheaton, IL: Crossway Books, 1994), 23–24.

17. Pearcey and Thaxton, *The Soul of Science*, 24.

By What Standard?

Those who control what young people are taught, and what they experience—what they see, hear, think, and believe—will determine the future course for the nation.[1]

ARCHIMEDES (287–212 B.C.), the Greek mathematician and physicist who yelled *Eureka!*—"I have found it!—as he ran naked from his bath tub at the discovery of the principle of displacement (Archimedes' Principle), once boasted that given the proper lever, and given a place to stand, he could "move the earth." But upon what would Archimedes stand to accomplish such a feat? Certainly not on the earth. Archimedes needed a place to stand *outside* the earth, a place *different* from the earth he wanted to move. Of course, his lever needed a fulcrum. This, too, had to rest on something.

Atlas of Greek Mythology (son of a Titan and brother of Prometheus), had a similar problem. Atlas was condemned by Zeus to stand eternally at the western end of the earth to hold up the sky. In art, however, Atlas is depicted as holding up the world. But what is Atlas using for his support of the earth? What is he standing upon?

Lance Morrow, writing for *Time* magazine, asks, "What are the chief American virtues now?"[2] William Bennett takes a stab at listing and supporting what he contends are the virtues that all people should emulate.[3] While *The Book of Virtues* is helpful, as we saw in the previous chapter, it lacks a certain and fixed ethical reference point. The following story points out the dilemma of modern man.

> A certain factory worker had the responsibility of blowing the whistle every day at precisely 12:00 noon. In order to be sure of the correct time, he set his own watch by a clock on the wall of a local jewelry store. After doing this for some time, it occurred to him that the jewelry story owner had to have some standard by which he could set his clock. Thus, one day when he was in the store, he inquired of the owner, "Sir, how do you know that time to set your clock?" The jewelry store owner replied, "Well, you see, on the other side of town there is a factory and every day precisely at noon they blow a whistle. . . ."[4]

Christians are often tempted to appeal to an authority not unlike themselves. If the Christian school is to thrive and survive, an appeal must be made to an authority outside of man.

All argumentation will inevitably be taken back to a single reference point from which the arguer will appeal for authority to support his worldview. That reference point, for example, might be the expert opinion of others. Of course, these experts are not the ultimate authorities. They also appeal to some decisive standard. "[J]ust because most of the authorities in a field are shouting in unison that they know the truth, it ain't necessarily so."[5] It is upon a final standard—a standard to which no greater appeal is made—that all worldviews rest.

> At the center of every world-view is what might be called the "touchstone proposition" of that world view, a proposition that is held to be *the* fundamental truth about reality and that serves as a criterion to determine which other propositions may or may not count as candidates for belief.[6]

The idea of a touchstone to establish authenticity, fineness, right and wrong, and justice is an old one. "In the days of the gold rush men used a touchstone, a fine grained dark stone, such as jasper, to determine the quality of the gold which they had discovered. Today a Geiger counter is used to locate uranium and other precious metals. In baseball the umpire makes the decisions in the contest between the pitcher and the batter. In the courtroom the judge decides questions of law. In their respective fields the touchstone, the Geiger counter, the umpire and the judge speak with authority."[7]

The development of an educational philosophy will always rest upon some ultimate standard of authority. For the Christian school that standard must be the Bible. Not the Bible *plus* something else. This does not mean that Christian teachers and students are indifferent to knowledge outside special revelation for we know that "the heavens are telling of the glory of God; and their expanse is declaring the work of His hands" (Ps. 19:1). It does mean that all knowledge must be filtered through the revelational format of the Bible.

We know that the created order, like man himself, is distorted. The creation now brings forth "thorns and thistles" (Gen. 3:18). God's special revelation is "perfect, restoring the soul; the testimony of the LORD is sure, making wise the simple" (Ps. 19:7). While the "grass withers and the flower fades . . . the word of our God stands forever" (Isa. 40:8).

At least four competing touchstone propositions will try to work their way into the authority structure of any Christian school: rationalism, empiricism, mysticism, and evidentialism.[8] While Christians cannot and should not deny the reality and usefulness of reason, experience, feelings, and evidences, all Christians must subordinate these competing authorities to the final authority of the Bible.

Notes

1. James C. Dobson, *Children at Risk*, 27. Quoted in Kimberly Blaker, "The Perils of Fundamentalism and the Imperilment of Democracy," *The Fundamentals of Extremism*: The Christian Right in America, ed. Kimberly Blaker (New Boston, MI: New Boston Books, Inc., 2003), 7: http://lostvegas.us/data/Fundamentals_of_Extremism-Ebook.pdf

2. Lance Morrow, "The Search for Virtues," *Time* (March 7, 1994), 78.

3. William J. Bennett, *The Book of Virtues* (New York: Simon & Schuster, 1993).

4. Quoted in Norman E. Harper, *Making Disciples: The Challenge of Christian Education at the End of the 20th Century* (Memphis, TN: Christian Studies Center, 1981), 5.

5. William R. Fix, *The Bone Peddlers: Selling Evolution* (New York: Macmillan, 1984), xix.

6. William H. Halverson, *A Concise Introduction to Philosophy*, 4th ed. (New York: McGraw-Hill, [1967] 1981), 414.

7. George M. Marston, *The Voice of Authority* (Nutley, NJ: Presbyterian and Reformed, 1960), xv.

8. Doug Powell, *Holman Quick Source Guide to Christian Apologetics* (Nashville, TN: Holman Reference, 2006), chap. 14.

5

A Comprehensive Biblical Worldview

When our Lord Jesus appeared, he acquired possession of the whole world; and his kingdom was extended from one end of it to the other, especially with the proclamation of the Gospel. . . . God has consecrated the entire earth through the precious blood of his Son to the end that we may inhabit it and live under his reign.[1]

MANY CHRISTIANS ARE still locked into the conviction that the Bible speaks to a very narrow slice of life. Of course, all Christians believe that the Bible has some very specific things to say about prayer, worship, and evangelism. But many Christians are not convinced that the Bible has some very definite things to say about civil government, the judicial system, economics, indebtedness, the punishment of criminals, foreign affairs, care for the poor, journalism, science, medicine, business, education, taxation, inflation, property, terrorism, war, peace negotiations, military defense, ethical issues like abortion and homosexuality, environmental concerns, inheritance, investments, building safety, banking, child discipline, pollution, marriage, contracts, and many other worldview issues including an education to teach these things from a biblical perspective.

Thinking God's Thoughts after Him

All Christians must remove their blinders and widen their scope of ministry to include the world. This will mean the development and implementation of a comprehensive biblical worldview. Put simply, a worldview is the way you and I look at things. How did we get here? How did the world get here? How does it run? Who or what runs it? What laws govern us and the world? What role if any do we have in the government of the world? What does God think of the world? How does He want it to run? Who has He put in charge of the world? What are His plans for the world? Basically, the Christian's worldview should be the same as God's worldview, the creature thinking the thoughts of the Creator.[2] Is God's view of the world comprehensive? Is He concerned about every nook and cranny of creation? Did He give His life for the "world"? Is He Lord of "all things"? To all of these questions we would answer "Yes!" Then why should Christians have a lower view of the world than God does? Why should humanists have a higher view of the world than Christians do?

> One of the basic demands of Christian discipleship, of following Jesus Christ, is to change our way of thinking. We are to "take captive every thought to make it obedient to Christ" (2 Corinthians 10:5). We are "not to be conformed to this world but [are to] be transformed by the renewing of our minds" (Romans 12:2). In other words, we are commanded to have a Biblical worldview. All our thinking, our perspective on life, and our understanding of the world around us, is to be comprehensively informed by Scripture.
>
> God's condemnation of Israel came because "their ways were not His ways and their thoughts were not His thoughts" (Isaiah 55:8). They did not have a Biblical worldview. When we begin to think about the law, or bio-medical ethics, or art, or business, or love, or history, or welfare, or anything else apart from God's revelation, we too have made ourselves vulnerable to condemnation. A Biblical worldview is not optional. It is mandatory.[3]

How does the Christian begin to develop a biblical worldview? Of course, the first place to start is with the Bible. The Bible is the blueprint for life. Just like a builder turns to his blueprints to build a house, the

Christian turns to the Bible to build a civilization that includes every area of life.

Because of the distortions of sin, we need a reliable standard to evaluate all of life. We cannot trust ourselves, the opinion of experts, the wishes of the majority, or "natural law" to be that standard. The Bible is our corrective lens for all of life. Man simply cannot be trusted. John Calvin said it well:

> Just as old or bleary-eyed men and those with weak vision, if you thrust before them a most beautiful volume, even if they recognize it to be some sort of writing, yet can scarcely construe two words, but with the aid of spectacles will begin to read distinctly; so Scripture, gathering up the otherwise confused knowledge of God in our minds, having dispersed our dullness, clearly shows us the true God.[4]

A lack of a comprehensive biblical worldview has left Christians open to a blind-side attack from humanists who have developed a comprehensive secular worldview. Non-Christians have no problem secularizing law, economics, ethics, journalism, education, politics, foreign affairs, and environmental issues. The sad thing is that many Christians believe that the steady secularization of every area of life is inevitable and that Christians should not involve themselves in the "Christianization" of every area of life. We, therefore, have witnessed the steady decline of the family, politics, education, and law, to name just a few.

False Spirituality

Failure to develop a comprehensive worldview often is related to a false view of spirituality. To be "spiritual" means to be governed by the Holy Spirit. For many, spirituality means to be preoccupied with non-physical reality. Therefore to be spiritual means not to be involved with the material things of this world.

> The unbiblical idea of "spirituality" is that the truly "spiritual" man is the person who is sort of "non-physical," who doesn't

get involved in "earthly" things, who doesn't work very much or
think very hard, and who spends most of his time meditating
about how he'd rather be in heaven. As long as he's on earth,
though, he has one main duty in life: Get stepped on for Jesus.
The "spiritual" man, in this view, is a wimp. A Loser. But at least
he's a *Good* Loser.[5]

The devil and his demons are spiritual (non-physical) and evil: "And I
saw coming out of the mouth of the dragon and out of the mouth of the
beast and out of the mouth of the false prophet, three *unclean spirits*
like frogs; for they are *spirits of demons*, performing signs, which go
out to the kings of the whole world, to gather them together for the war
of the great day of God Almighty" (Rev. 16:13–14). There are "deceitful
spirits" (1 Tim. 4:1), "unclean spirits" (Rev. 18:2), and spirits of "error" (1
John 4:6). There is even "spiritual wickedness" (Eph. 6:12).

On the other hand, Jesus has a body and He is good: "For David, after
he had served the purpose of God in his own generation, fell asleep, and
was laid among his fathers, and underwent decay; *but He whom God
raised did not undergo decay*" (Acts 13:36–37). Jesus was raised with His
body. He is "the Holy and Righteous One" (Acts 3:14). Spirituality is directly related to righteousness. The reason Jesus' body did not undergo
decay was because He was without sin.

There is the "Holy Spirit" (e.g., Acts 13:2), a "spirit of truth" (1 John
4:6), "spiritual things" (1 Cor. 9:11), "spiritual food" (10:3), a "spiritual
body" (15:44), "spiritual sacrifices" (1 Peter 2:5), "spiritual wisdom and
understanding" (Col. 1:9), and "ministering spirits, sent out to render
service for the sake of those who will inherit salvation" (Heb. 1:14).

To be "spiritual" is to exhibit the "gifts of the Spirit" (Gal. 5:22).
We are told to "walk in the spirit" (5:16). But how does a Christian know when he or she is walking "in the spirit"?

To be Spiritual is to be guided and motivated by the Holy Spirit. It means obeying His commandments as recorded in Scriptures. The Spiritual man is not someone who floats in midair and
hears eerie voices. The Spiritual man is the man who does what
the Bible says (Rom. 8:4–8). This means, therefore, that we *are* to

get involved in life. God wants us to apply Christian standards everywhere, in every way. Spirituality does not mean retreat and withdrawal from life; it means *dominion*. The basic Christian confession of faith is that *Jesus* is Lord (Rom. 10:9–10)—Lord of all things, in heaven and on earth.[6]

The commandments of God are the rules by which we measure our spirituality. We are told that the "Law is spiritual" (Romans 7:14). Notice also that the spiritual person "appraises [judges] *all things*" (2:15). The reason he can judge all things is because he has an inerrant, infallible, God-breathed Book (2 Tim. 3:16–17).

The Bible does not support the belief that Christians should abandon the world because the world is not "spiritual." Rather, Christians are to transform the world through the power of the Spirit, using the spiritual Law of God as the standard of righteousness for appraising (judging) where regeneration and restoration are needed. Christians are to be "salt" and "light" *in* the world (Matt. 5:13–14). Salt is useless unless applied to a potentially decaying world; light is not needed unless there is darkness to scatter (5:15; Luke 2:32). Without involvement in the world, salt and light are not needed. Christians are to be in the world, but they are not to be of the world (John 17:14–16). They are not to be squeezed into the world's mold (Rom. 12:2). They are not to be led astray by the "elementary principles of the world" (Col. 2:8). They are to keep themselves "unstained by the world" (James 1:27). They are warned not to get entangled in the "defilements of the world" (2 Peter 2:20). Nowhere are they told to abandon the world (cf. Matt. 28:18–20; John 3:16).

The "world" is corrupt because people are corrupt. Where corrupt people control certain aspects of the world we can expect defilement. But the world does not have to remain in decay. When individuals are redeemed, the effects of their redemption should spread to the society in which they live and conduct their affairs.

Could one properly say that a Christian operating a business according to biblical laws should allow himself and his business to be squeezed into the world's mold, stained by the world, defiled, and led astray? Cer-

tainly not! We would encourage other businessmen to follow his example of transforming and restoring all their business dealings. The world
of pagan thinking and practice is to be replaced by Christian thinking
and practice. It is a perversion of the gospel to maintain that the world,
as the domain where evil exists, is inherently corrupt. We should remember that Jesus came to this world to give His life for its redemption
(John 3:16). Christians must be transformed by God's word and not be
conformed to the world's principles. As Christians work in the world
through the power of the Holy Spirit, the world will be transformed.

By denying the spirituality of God's created order, we neglect its importance and give it by default to those who deny Christ. *Worldliness* is
to be avoided, not the world. The Bible warns

> against worldliness *wherever* it is found [James 1:27], certainly in
> the church, and he is emphasizing here precisely the importance
> of Christian involvement in *social* issues. Regrettably, we tend
> to read the Scriptures as though their rejection of a "worldly"
> life-style entails a recommendation of an "otherworldly" one.
>
> This approach has led many Christians to abandon the "secu-
> lar" realm to the trends and forces of secularism. Indeed, because
> of their two-realm theory, to a large degree, Christians have
> themselves to blame for the rapid secularization of the West. If
> political, industrial, artistic, and journalistic life, to mention only
> these areas, are branded as essentially "worldly," "secular," "pro-
> fane," and part of the "natural domain of creaturely life," then is it
> surprising that Christians have not more effectively stemmed the
> tide of humanism in our culture?[7]

God created everything wholly good (Gen. 1:31). Man, through the fall,
became profane, defiled by sin. Redemption restores things in Christ.
Peter failed to understand the gospel's comprehensive cleansing effects. He could not believe the Gentiles were "clean": "What God has
cleansed, no longer consider unholy" (Acts 10:15; cf. Matt. 15:11; Rom.
14:14, 20). The fall did not nullify God's pronouncement that the created order "was very good" (Gen. 1:31). The New Testament reinforces
the goodness of God's creation: "For everything created by God is good,

and nothing is to be rejected, if it is received with gratitude; for it is sanctified by means of the word of God and prayer" (1 Tim. 4:4–5).

Scripture is our guide and not the Platonic view of matter as something less than good. God "became flesh and dwelt among us" (John 1:14). Jesus worked in his earthly father's shop as a carpenter, affirming the goodness of the created order and the value of physical labor.

Notes

1. John Calvin quoted in William J. Bouwsma, *John Calvin: A Sixteenth Century Portrait* (New York: Oxford University Press, 1988), 192

2. Johannes Kepler (1571–1630) wrote: "O God, I am thinking thy thoughts after thee." Quoted in Charles E. Hummel, *The Galileo Connection: Resolving Conflicts between Science and the Bible* (Downers Grove, IL: InterVarsity Press, 1986), 57. The worldviews of Christians, humanists, New Agers, Socialists, and Marxists are built on religious presuppositions. For a presentation of the presuppositional model see Gary DeMar, *Thinking Straight in a Crooked World* (Powder Springs, GA: American Vision, 2001) and Gary DeMar, ed., *Pushing the Antithesis: The Apologetic Methodology of Greg L. Bahnsen* (Powder Springs, GA: American Vision, 2007).

3. George Grant, *Bringing in the Sheaves: Transforming Poverty into Productivity* (Atlanta, GA: American Vision, 1985), 93. The worldview of Christianity is always at war with all other worldviews and their implications for life: "Joseph Fletcher describes the clash of value systems, or world views most starkly. On the one hand is a 'simplistic' view which holds that 'living and dying are in God's hands and that life is God's to give and only God's to take.' On the other us 'humanistic medicine,' with its ethic of responsibility, including 'responsibility for the termination of subhuman life in posthuman beings.'" (James Manney, "Rationalizing Infanticide: Medical Ethics in the Eighties," Carl Horn, ed., *Whose Values?: The Battle for Morality in a Pluralistic America* [Ann Arbor, MI: Servant Books, 1985], 102).

4. John T. McNeill, ed., *Institutes of the Christian Religion* (Philadelphia, PA: Westminster Press, 1960), Book I, chapter 2, section 1.

5. David Chilton, *Paradise Restored* (Tyler, TX: Institute for Christian Economics, 1985), 3–4.

6. Chilton, *Paradise Restored*, 4.

7. Albert M. Wolters, *Creation Regained: Biblical Basics for a Reformational Worldview* (Grand Rapids, MI: Eerdmans, 1985), 54.

6

Why the Future Matters

You see, the way you look to the future determines your planning and your actions. It is the way you understand the times that determines what you are going to do.[1]

WHEN ISRAEL WAS taken to the borders of the promised land, twelve spies were called on to survey the land and report their findings to the nation (Num. 13). Before choosing twelve representatives for the task, God *promised* the land would be theirs: "Send out for yourself men so that they may spy out the land of Canaan, which *I am going to give to the sons of Israel*; you shall send a man from each of their fathers' tribes, every one a leader among them" (13:2). No matter what the spies encountered, the *promise* of God should have had priority and overruled any desire to retreat. When the spies returned, ten brought back pessimistic (unbelieving) reports (13:28–29, 31–33). Two spies, Joshua and Caleb, returned with optimistic reports because they believed God and not the fears of men, nor the circumstances they encountered (13:30). It is important to note that Caleb never denied that there were "giants in the land," he simply believed that God was stronger (obviously) than any army of giants. Why is this so?: "You are from God, little children, and have overcome them; because greater is He that is in you than he who is in the world" (1 John 4:4).

The nation responded to the report without faith. In effect, they called God a liar: "Then all the congregation lifted up their voices and cried, and the people wept that night" (14:1). Their refusal to believe the promise of God (cf. 13:2) brought judgment upon the entire nation. Israel did not enter the promised land until forty years passed and the unbelieving generation died (14:26–38). Their pessimistic perspective of the future affected their plans for the future. The task of dominion was seen as too great for God, hence too great for man under God's providence. Instead of moving forward they chose retreat to the past: "Would that we had died in the land of Egypt! Or would that we had died in the wilderness! And why is the LORD bringing us into this land, to fall by the sword? Our wives and our little ones will become plunder; would it not be better for us to return to Egypt? So they said to one another, 'Let us appoint a leader and return to Egypt'" (14:2–4).

A pessimistic faith ruins Christian dominion. Israel lost forty years of dominion because the nation trusted the words of men and the circumstances of the world more than the word of God. When Israel entered the land forty years later, Rahab told the two unnamed spies what the inhabitants were thinking: "For we have heard how the LORD dried up the water of the Red Sea before you when you came out of Egypt, and what you did to the two kings of the Amorites who were beyond the Jordan, to Sihon and Og, whom you utterly destroyed. And when we heard it, *our hearts melted and no courage remained in any man any longer because of you*" (Josh. 2:10–11). The Canaanites looked upon the Israelites, at the time Israel was freed from Egyptian bondage over forty years before, as the giants. Forty years of dominion were wasted because Israel failed to trust the God who possesses the future (and controls the present in order to fulfill His plan for the future).

Plant Some Oak Trees

The Christian's view of the future determines how he lives and works in the present.[2] If he believes the future to be bleak, his pessimism will be reflected in a variety of ways, usually in inactivity. The family will not be trained to consider the wider aspects of dominion as they relate to successive generations. Education will be present-oriented, with students obtaining an education merely to secure the necessary credentials for a job. While Christians might establish schooling for children in grades 1–12, very little will be done to set up colleges, universities, and graduate schools to prepare *generations* of Christians to influence their professions, nation, and world for Christ. One reason students find it difficult to apply themselves in school is their inability to see how their academic work translates into meaningful preparation for the future. It was not always this way. Students believed that their work in the classroom would by necessity translate into the refinement of their calling under God for the fulfilling of the Great Commission and the advancement of God's kingdom as this story demonstrates:

> New College, Oxford, is of rather late foundation, hence the name. It was probably founded around the late 16th century. It has, like other colleges, a great dining hall with big oak beams across the top, yes? These might be eighteen inches square, twenty feet long.
>
> Some five to ten years ago, so I am told, some busy entomologist went up into the roof of the dining hall with a penknife and poked at the beams and found that they were full of beetles. This was reported to the College Council, who met in some dismay, because where would they get beams of that caliber nowadays?
>
> One of the Junior Fellows stuck his neck out and suggested that there might be on the College lands some oak. These colleges are endowed with pieces of land scattered across the country. So they called the College Forester, who of course had not been near the college itself for some years, and asked him about the oaks.
>
> And he pulled his forelock and said, "Well sirs, we was wonderin' when you'd be askin'."
>
> Upon further inquiry it was discovered that when the College was founded, a grove of oaks had been planted to replace the beams in the dining hall when they became beetly, because oak beams always become beetly in the end. This plan had been passed down from one Forester to the next for four hundred years. "You don't cut them oaks. Them's for the College Hall." A nice story. That's a way to run a culture.[3]

Reform the World

For too long, Christians have believed that the future should be considered only in terms of heaven or the events that lead to the second coming of Jesus Christ. Events and concerns about the time "in between" have been regarded of little real importance. Because of this false idea, many Christians abdicate their responsibilities toward education, economics, science, and civil government. Any study of these disciplines is purely utilitarian. A mollified eschatology has accelerated the debilitating effects of a belief system that teaches as biblical orthodoxy that the end of all things is near, leading to further inactivity on the part of God's people. God instructed His people to reform the world, not preach a doctrine of prophetic inevitability:

> The apostle Paul had to rebuke some of the Thessalonians for ceasing to work simply because of the possibility that the Lord might return immediately. Christians since then have often been notorious for embracing escapist attitudes toward work due to their eschatologies [doctrine of the last things]. Rather than aggressively moving forward to take dominion over the earth, the Church has all too often lapsed into an irresponsible passivity, approaching her commission with the attitude: "You don't polish brass on a sinking ship." Jesus, however, instructed us to take the opposite approach. In the parable of the ten minas (Luke 19:11–27), the master gave each of his servants money and told them, "*Do business with this* until I come back." In this story, Jesus commands us to take the offensive and "do business" until He returns.[4]

The biblical view of the future presents the truth that history is moving forward, and every Christian is responsible before God to show himself a good and faithful steward of his God-given gifts. God requires an accounting.

The kingdom of God has purpose because God directs its every movement. History is not bound by a never-ending series of cycles, with God powerless to intervene and govern. The future, as Nebuchadnezzar came to realize, is governed by God. Earthly sovereigns who fail to recognize God's absolute sovereignty will be destroyed: "You [Nebuchadnezzar] continued looking [at the statue] until a stone was cut out without hands, and it struck the statue on its feet of iron and clay, and crushed them. Then the iron, the clay, the bronze, the silver and the gold were crushed all at the same time, and became like chaff from the summer threshing floors; and the wind carried them away so that not a trace of them was found. But the stone that struck the statue became a great mountain and filled the whole earth" (Dan. 2:34–35). The pagan idea of the future is a myth. The future belongs to God's people and Christians are not trapped in futile historical cycles.

The Christian's view of the future determines how he lives, plans, and works in the present *for the future.* Even during Israel's captivity under Babylonian rule, the nation's darkest hour, the people were told to plan and build for the future: "Build houses and live in them; and plant gardens, and eat their produce. Take wives and become the fathers of sons and daughters, and take wives for your sons and give your daughters to husbands, that they may bear sons and daughters; and multiply there and do not decrease. . . . For I know the plans that I have for you, 'declares the LORD,' plans for welfare and not for calamity to give you a future and a hope" (Jer. 29:5–6, 11).

God's words seemed contrary to what people saw all around them. Destruction and captivity awaited the nation, yet God commanded them to prepare for the *future.* In spite of every pessimistic view, God wanted the people's desires and hopes to be future-directed. Build for what will be. The psychological benefit of such a mind set does much to spur the church of Jesus Christ to greater kingdom activity. A preoccupation with defeat brings defeat by default. Why would anyone wish to build for the future when there is no earthly future hope? Who would invest in a losing proposition? Why should anyone work to establish a godly home, school, business, or civil government when all such institutions seemed doomed despite our efforts?

"We must become *optimists* concerning the victory that lies before Christ's people, in time and on earth. We must be even more optimistic than Joshua and Caleb, for they were only asked to spy out the land of Canaan. They were called to give their report prior to Christ's sacrifice at

Calvary. Why should we be pessimistic, like that first generation of former slaves? Why should we wander in the wilderness, generation after generation? Why should we despair?"[5] The hope of the future is real because Christians should know that God governs the affairs of men and nations (Ps. 22:28; 47:8; 127:1; Dan. 4:35). All conspiracies, no matter how well planned, will be put to an end by the God who rules from heaven (Ps. 2).

Progress for the Faithful

The Apostle Paul informs Timothy "that in the last days difficult times will come" (2 Tim. 3:1). The ungodly will manifest a variety of characteristics which evidence their opposition to God's purposes: "For men will be lovers of self, lovers of money, boastful, arrogant, evildoers, disobedient to parents, ungrateful, unholy, etc." (3:2–5). Timothy is told to "avoid such men as these" (3:5).

Will the ungodly dominate culture? At first reading, 2 Timothy 3 would seem to indicate that the ungodly will prevail, and godly influence decline. Further study shows that the Apostle Paul is describing a different scenario. Paul compares the progress of the ungodly in Timothy's day with that of Jannes and Jambres, the Egyptian sorcerer-priests who opposed Moses (cf. Ex. 7:11): "But they will not make further progress; for their folly will be obvious to all, as also that of those two came to be" (2 Tim. 3:9). While it is true there is an *attempt* by the ungodly to dominate culture, the fact is, "they will not make further progress"; their fling with ungodliness is only temporary (cf. Rom. 1:18–32). The Christian can remain optimistic even if ungodly actions increase. In time, if Christians remain faithful in influencing their world with the gospel, actions of the ungodly will be eliminated.

Paul, however, does not allow the Christian to remain passive as the ungodly self-destruct. Timothy has followed Paul's "teaching, conduct, purpose, faith, patience, love, perseverance, persecutions, [and] sufferings" (2 Tim. 3:10–11) and he calls on us to do the same (3:16–17). While the ungodly expend their spiritual capital in present-oriented living, and, therefore, have nothing saved for the future, the Christian is to develop future-oriented spiritual capital to replace the bankrupt culture of humanism with a Christ-centered society. Notice that the characteristics of the ungodly are all self-directed and short-lived, summarized by this phrase: "lovers of pleasure rather than lovers of God" (3:4). Sin has its pleasure for a short period of time: "He who loves pleasure will become a poor man; he who loves wine and oil will not become rich" (Prov. 21:17). The love of pleasure is no investment in the future.

The characteristics of the godly are future directed, foregoing the lure of present pleasures for the benefit of future productivity. Teaching, conduct, purpose, faith, patience, love and perseverance take time and energy from the present, but result in future reward. For example, the farmer could consume all of his harvested grain in a year's time and have none to plant for the following year. By consuming just enough grain to feed his family and storing reserves for a potential poor crop along with some for planting, he guarantees his family security and a dominion status for the future.

While the present-oriented consumer furiously looks for a way to feed his family, the future-oriented farmer spends his free time exercising godly dominion in his culture. Moreover, persecutions and sufferings should not deter the future-oriented Christian because "out of them all the Lord" delivers us (2 Tim. 3:11). In the same way, the future-oriented farmer can overcome the effects of a bad harvest because his store allows him to live until the next harvest. The effects of a bad harvest for the present-oriented consumer is disastrous. With no reserves, he possesses no hope for the future.

If the Christian looks only at present happenings he loses his hope of becoming a cultural influence, since he perceives the statement, "evil men and impostors will proceed from bad to worse, deceiving and being deceived" (2 Tim. 3:13) as something permanent. But we also must remember the previous words of Paul: "But they will not make further progress; for their folly will be obvious to all" (3:9). In the short-term, it appears that the ungodly will prevail. Christians, however, must begin to think long-term; while the ungodly burn themselves out, the godly steadily influence their world: "You, however, *continue* in the things you have learned and become convinced of" (3:14). In time, the effects of dominion will be seen: "And let us not lose heart in doing good, for in due time we shall reap if we do not grow weary" (Gal. 6:9). The goal is to outlast and outwork those who have as their goal the dispossession of God's kingship over them.

Notes

1. Josef Ton, "The Cornerstone at the Crossroads," *Wheaton Alumni* (August/ September 1991), 6–7.

2. For a thorough study of eschatology (study of the last things), see Gary DeMar, *Last Days Madness: Obsession of the Modern Church*, 4th ed. (Powder Springs, GA: American Vision, 1999). For a survey of the issue, see Gary DeMar, *Is Jesus Coming Soon?* (Powder Springs, GA: American Vision, 2006).

3. Gregory Bateson, "The Oak Beams of New College, Oxford," *The Next Whole Earth Catalog*, 2nd ed. (New York: Rand McNally, 1981), 77.

4. Joseph McAuliffe, "Do Business Until I Return," *New Wine* (January 1982), 29.

5. Gary North, *Unconditional Surrender*, 2nd ed. (Tyler, TX: Geneva Press, 1983), 214.

Part II

7

Setting the Agenda

[T]he school must seek to develop increasingly its freedom from and independence of state controls, state standards, and state accreditation. The root word in accreditation is credo, 'I believe.' If the state is our Lord, it is the state's approval and imprimatur we seek. If Christ is our Lord, it is the accreditation of His word we seek.[1]

THE FIRST TWO questions that a prospective parent asks about a new school is: Are the teachers certified and is the school accredited? No one asks if Harvard, Yale, and Princeton are accredited and its professors certified by civil officials. The reason for this is quite simple: Harvard, Yale, and Princeton are readily accepted because they are prestigious institutions that have a perceived reputation of quality. All other educational institutions are measured by the standards of these academic establishments.[2]

Christian institutions, in order to be accepted by the educational establishment and the broader culture, believe that an academic stamp of approval is necessary in order to compete. How will people know that a school measures up if it is not accredited? But why was the new school started in the first place? Is not the main purpose of a Christian institution to counter the anti-Christian worldview of existing institutions? Why turn to the very agencies that are working for our destruction and seek their approval for our work? Philosophical independence must be maintained by the Christian school.

The very same people who Christians regard as anti-Christian in their social and educational philosophies have set up the accreditation system, and the Christian school movement has rushed to submit itself to them in order to get their certification of academic acceptability. Acquiescence to accreditation and certification efforts on humanist terms is suicidal.

Accreditation and certification guidelines have been used by the political left to capture the robes of Christian academia. Schools, even Christian schools, are most often evaluated in terms of how many PhDs serve on the faculty. Studies show that "theology faculty who hold the rank of PhD are more liberal on every social and political issue measured . . . than are those with other academic degree experience. . . ."[3] Similar surveys show that a comparable trend exists in the social science fields.

The school should not seek accreditation of its program or certification of its teachers from outside agencies. Accreditation should be established by the school to be used as a standard for other schools. Teacher certification is not a test of competency.[4] If it were, our nation's public schools would be the best in the world. The school should develop a system whereby a prospective teacher goes through a training program which results in certification *by the school*.

Kingdom Missionary Academies

Each year our church holds a Missions Conference. A few years ago, a missionary from West Africa gave a stirring account of how a school had been built to educate the young people and prepare adults for indigenous missionary work. The parents saw the school as a means to a better life for their children. So while the parents spent the day working to stay alive, their children would spend a few hours at school. The missionaries set up the school as a way to present the gospel as well as to introduce them to a broader education. Once the children became literate, they could read the Bible and basic theological primers, both in English and their own language if a translation was available. Once the children could read the Bible, they would take their child-like understanding of God's Word home to their parents. Many parents would come to know Christ by way of their children.

I watched the expressions on the faces of the people in our Sunday school class as they heard these wonderful stories about how so many otherwise unreached people were hearing the gospel. They were excited enough actually to donate to the building of more of these schools. It's such a simple and practical strategy, the Great Commission at work.

So why isn't this strategy used in America? Why not erect Kingdom Academies in areas where the unsaved need a place to put their children during the day as they head off to work? Many women don't have the luxury to stay at home with their children. They have to work, for any number of reasons that escape many of us. They might be divorced or abandoned by their husband. Maybe they are escaping an abusive spouse. Some might be single mothers who are trying to better themselves, and a job is a prime necessity. We rant and rave about the evils of abortion, as we should, but when women must work and have a place to put their child while they are on the job, we reject the idea of day care, even if it's Christian. It really doesn't matter what the reason is as to why they must work; they need a safe environment for their children until quitting time. Why do so few Christians see this as a missionary opportunity? I don't get it.

And what about Christian mothers who find themselves in a similar position where they must work, again, for whatever reason? What choices do they have? They have to work to care for their children. Wouldn't it be great if there were Christian day care establishments that offered a truly biblical curriculum where children learned to read by the age of three, studied the Bible, memorized Scripture verses, had a stable and disciplined daily routine taught to them, and then went home as changed little boys and girls? When mom or dad asked, "And what did you learn in school today," they would get an earful, an earful of the gospel!

How is setting up Christian day care centers—I prefer to call them "Kingdom Academies"—different from building schools in Africa so the gospel can be made available to young people so parents might hear as well? It's not. The church is missing out on a missionary opportunity literally in its back yard. Some of these children will drag their parents to church. When these children reach the age to enter the first grade, many parents will want to continue the education that these Kingdom Academies began. Church Sunday school rooms are vacant six days a week. This is a waste of the tithe if the rooms are not being fully utilized. They should be used for educating our children instead of sending them to educational facilities controlled by the State. Churches that establish Kingdom Academies will have a steady supply of students to continue the work begun in them. Unlike Timothy, many young parents didn't have a faithful grandmother and mother who instilled a "sincere faith within" them (2 Tim. 1:5), and as a result, they don't have a mature faith to instill in their own children.

If you want to change the world, change the children. How can teaching children to read and taking them through the Bible five days a week be a bad thing, especially when most families, Christian ones included, don't do it?

Notes

1. Rousas J. Rushdoony, *The Philosophy of the Christian School Curriculum* (Vallecito, CA: Ross House Books, 1981), 142–143.

2. The evaluation is made in terms of humanistic categories.

3. Ladd and Ferre, *This World* (Summer 1992), 86.

4. Teachers at Westminster Schools in Atlanta, Georgia, are not state certified. Isn't it curious that college and university professors are not certified and yet they instruct prospective teachers who must be certified in order to teach in state institutions?

8

Balaam's Donkey has Spoken

There is no one underlying set of assumptions that guides the moral life of American children.[1]

I BELIEVE GOD HAS been giving us a very clear message through the modern-day equivalent of Balaam's donkey: The United States Supreme Court and nearly every lower court. Balaam was called on by Balak, the king of Moab, to prophesy against Israel. God had warned Balaam to stay away from Moab. Balaam refused. The Angel of the Lord met Balaam on the road as he was going down to meet Balak. Balaam's donkey refused to confront the Angel of the LORD. Balaam struck his donkey three times to force him ahead. Finally, Balaam realized that it was the Lord who was directing him to turn around.

Repeatedly the Supreme Court has ruled against Christians and their attempts to bring prayer, Bible reading, and even a cursory mention of a Creator back to the classroom. Like Balaam, a majority of Christians refuse to heed the message that God is giving them through the Court: Seek a different route.

Saying prayers at sporting events, reciting "under God" in the Pledge of Allegiance, praying around a flag pole once a year, and having the right to "a moment of silence" do not constitute a Christian education. The entire curriculum must be Christ-centered. God is speaking to us through the Court: "Get your children out of the schools that deny Me!" Do we have the sense to listen to what God is telling us?

Students in public schools are often denied the right to discuss religion except in a multi-cultural way. If Christianity is discussed, it can only be studied in the context of other religious belief systems in their historical setting. But as we've seen, even this approach is no longer accepted in reference to Christianity. Steven Williams, a fifth-grade teacher at Stevens Creek School in the San Francisco Bay area suburb of Cupertino, was barred by his school from giving students documents from American history that refer to God, including the Declaration of Independence which establishes the basis of our rights in that they are an endowment from the Creator and not a gift from the State.[2]

Criticism of evolution is forbidden in most public (government) educational institutions, even if the discussion is solely academic. The claim is made that behind the criticism lurks religious presuppositions. Abstinence education also falls into this category.[3]

Christians want to believe that "academic freedom" is an operating principle in academic settings, so they push for "equal time for Jesus" or the two-model approach to teaching origins. Academic freedom is a one-way street. The notion of academic freedom is used by secularists to persuade Christians to open their educational establishments to non-Christian teachers who can teach so-called neutral subjects like science, music, and math[4] where religion is irrelevant. The greatest scientists and mathematicians did not make a division between religion and knowledge. "Nicholaus Copernicus (1473–1543), the Polish astronomer, marveled when he observed the land of God in the correlation between mathematical thought and the actions of nature. To him, the universe was 'wrought for us by a supremely good and orderly Creator.' He lauded the Creator in praise, 'So great is this divine work of the Great and Noble Creator.'"[5] Harvard was lost when it separated the religion department from the academic departments on the assumption that knowledge is neutral.[6] There is no such open-door policy in secular institutions. Public schools are no exception. Are we surprised when public schools act consistent with their adopted secularist worldview?

We shouldn't be. He who pays the piper calls the tune; he who collects your tax dollars by force develops and enforces the curriculum. When will Christians understand this?

Why do Christians waste time, money, and their children in defense of public (government) education? While Christians attempt to "save" their beloved local public schools, another generation of young people is seduced by the anti-Christian worldview of a materialist education. This has been happening for decades with no progress. Public schools aren't even what they were in the 1960s. Watch *Mr. Holland's Opus*[7]— which follows the career of a school's music teacher from 1965 to 1995— and *Lean on Me* to see the retrogression.[8]

The no-public-education view isn't popular with the majority of Christians. Blasting public education in America is for some akin to blaspheming on holy ground. What would communities do without their high school sports teams and their "free" education? In order to justify the continued support of public—government—education, the following excuses are often given:

"We can't afford to send our children to private schools."

If Christians pulled their children out of public schools, voted down every tax increase having to do with education, repealed the education portion of the property tax, and supported candidates who would cut every dollar from education funding, then most families could afford the costs involved. The money spent on trying to "save" public schools would go a long way to establish scholarship funds for families who cannot afford a private-school education. Yes, it may even take some sacrificing on the part of some. Of course, home schooling is always an option. Drive a fourteen-year-old car like I did while my wife and I sent our children to non-government schools. Live in a smaller house. Don't eat out as much. There are many ways to cut spending to fund the real necessities of life. When your children get older, have them work to share the financial load.

"Only a few things need to be fixed."

Laura Mallory is a concerned mother of three. She wants the Harry Potter books removed from the library of J.C. Magill Elementary School in
the Gwinnett County, Georgia, public school system where her children
attend because she says the books, which have world-wide sales of more
than 300 million, glorify witchcraft. Mallory first took her complaint to
the county school board in September 2005. In May of 2006, the board
decided that the books should remain in the library. Malloy then took
her concerns to the state board where a decision will be made some-
time in December. Here is an indication of her naïveté, believing that if
Harry Potter is banished all will be right in the public schools and that
the schools and all the teachers have the best worldview interests of her
children at heart: "When my children are at school, I'm trusting them
to the teachers and that school. They are my most precious things in
the entire world to me. I surely don't want them indoctrinated into a
religion whose practices are evil."[9]

She has embarked on a fool's errand. I'm always amazed when I read
stories about well-intentioned parents who want this book removed or
that course dropped as if these minor changes will result in an educational reformation. It's not going to happen. The sooner parents
learn this, the sooner they will save their children from things worse
than witchcraft—like the belief that public education is a neutral endeavor designed to equip young people to be objective learners. Based
on what the courts have decided over the years, the public schools are
"religious (Christian)-free zones." In a word, they are officially atheistic. You would think that most Christian parents would be concerned
about this. They're not. They continue to believe that public education
can be saved. It can't. Mrs. Mallory is spitting in the wind when she
doesn't have to. Her children are being co-opted everyday by a more
subtle type of witchcraft, the "philosopher's stone" of the magic-laden
and irrational worldview of materialism. Her children are being taught
that they've descended from animals, that they are animals. "When it
comes to DNA," the people at *Time* magazine tell us, "a human is closer
to a chimp than a mouse is to a rat."[10] This is first-rate paganism. Gone is

the belief that we are endowed by our "Creator with certain inalienable rights." This concerned mother is more concerned with what sits on the library shelves than what is actually being taught in the classroom.

Public schools have become the new worldview battleground. Christians are fighting on the enemy's soil when they should be building their own educational kingdom. Harry Potter is a symptom of a larger crisis that is easily fixed if parents take the responsibility of educating their own children and refuse to turn them over to the State for secular propagandizing.

"It's not the church's job to educate."

I've heard this one a lot. Christian school critics balk at turning over the church's facilities for educational purposes because the tithe is designed to support the church's work, not the education of children. "That's why we pay taxes." The church building is vacant six days a week. Sunday school classrooms are used for forty-five minutes a week! What a waste of God's money. Our church supports numerous missionaries. Many of the missionaries we support build schools in foreign lands. Why is it OK to build schools in Africa, South America, or China with our tithe but not in our own backyard?

So we send our children to public schools where they are indoctrinated for thirty hours of classroom instruction each week in the latest non-Christian propaganda. To combat secularized education, Christian-school critics develop "youth programs" for Wednesday and Sunday evenings. These kids are getting at most two hours of weekly second-rate religious instruction, while a child in a Christian school receives thirty hours of training from a biblical perspective. There's no comparison. Most church "youth programs" are entertainment gatherings with a "devotional" to give them legitimacy.

When I attended Catholic school, there was no Sunday school instruction. The assumption was that religious instruction was woven into the daily educational curriculum. When my parents sent me to public school in the sixth grade, I had to attend religious instruction on Saturday morning to make up the deficiency. There is no way that the 45-minute instruction period could compensate for what I was not receiving at the local public school.

"My child is a witness for Christ in the public schools."

He or she may be. But I wonder how much witnessing actually takes place in public schools. Most of the time children are sitting at their desks listening to a teacher lecturing on a secularized curriculum. From the time I entered public school in the sixth grade, no one ever presented the gospel to me. It's the friendships that are developed after school that lead to witnessing opportunities. Witnessing can take place anywhere. Jesus met people at work and in their homes. He even went into the temple. If you want to follow Jesus' example then go witness to Jews in their local temples. Jesus never witnessed in a school.

"Our school is different."

I heard this one from the head of a prominent Christian ministry. I told him that it's a common response. In fact, as much as I hear it told, it seems that no one's school is bad. It's always some other community's school system that's in need of reform. My guess is that most parents have no idea what's going on in their child's school. If they don't hear any bad news, they assume that all is well. Keep in mind that public school children are not comparing their education with the public school education that was prominent forty years ago. And it wasn't that great back then. The education students are receiving right now is normal for them. It's the only standard they know, and it's not a very good one. Anyway, a school that does not teach from a Christian perspective is at best third-rate and dangerous.

"I want my child to be exposed to the 'real' world."

Who defines what constitutes the "real world"? The real world is where Christ dwells and where His Word is taught. Christianity is not unreal. If it is, then why not worship with pagans since their domain is the "real world." Remember, Adam and Eve "fell" from what was normal, that is, from a world where they were in intimate fellowship with their Creator. A world without Christ is an insane and irrational world. The Christian school is a place of re-creation, a redemptive attempt to get back to the original design while still acknowledging that we are fallen creatures. Schools that Christians establish should act as magnets for unbelievers to be brought back to the garden. Christians should be setting the agenda for what's real, honest, and good so as to be a light for those who are in darkness.

The Slide to Official Atheism Continues

What has to take place in the public schools before Christians will finally say enough is enough? The courts continue to put up road blocks for any type reform. When the Cobb County, Georgia, school board wanted to place a sticker on biology books stating that "evolution is a theory, not a fact, regarding the origin of living things" and that the study of the subject "should be approached with an open mind,"[11] Christians rejoiced, the ACLU sued and won, the stickers were removed, and the continued secularization of the government-controlled schools progressed. Was there a mass exodus by Christian students? Were there demonstations in the streets? Christians protest when they see and hear about the seasonal war on Christmas, but they seem indifferent to the fact that there is a daily war for the heart and mind of their own children.

Notes

1. Joan Connell, "American Children are Becoming Moral Illiterates," *Marietta Daily Journal* (October 11, 1990), 5B.

2. www.thesmokinggun.com/archive/1124041declar1.html

3. www.plannedparenthood.org/library/facts/AbstinenceOnly10-01.html

4. On the non-neutral foundation of mathematics, see Vern Poythress, "A Biblical View of Mathematics," *Foundations of Christian Scholarship*, ed. Gary North (Vellecito, CA: Ross House Books, 1976), 159–188.

5. James Nickel, *Mathematics: Is God Silent?* (Vallecito, CA: Ross House Books, 1990).

6. Samuel L. Blumenfeld, *Is Public Education Necessary?* (Old Greenwich, CT: The Devin-Adair Co., 1981).

7. www.filethirteen.com/reviews/mrholland/mrholland.htm

8. www.americanrhetoric.com/MovieSpeeches/moviespeechleanonme3.html

9. Laura Diamond, "Mom: Ban Potter (Hogwarts and all)," *The Atlanta Journal-Constitution* (October 4, 2006), D8.

10. Michael D. Lemonick and Andrea Dorfman, "What Makes Us Different?," *Time* (October 9, 2006), 46.

11. Diance R. Stepp and Kristina Torres, "Cobb gives up on evolution book stickers," *The Atlanata Journal-Constitution* (December 20, 2006), A1, 14.

9

The Moral Heirs of Epicurus

If the solar system was brought about by an accidental collision,
then the appearance of organic life on this planet was also an ac-
cident, and the whole evolution of Man was an accident too. If so,
then all our thought processes are mere accidents—the accidental
by-product of the movement of atoms. And this holds for the ma-
terialists' and astronomers' as well as for anyone else's [thought
processes]. But if their thoughts—i.e., of Materialism and Astron-
omy—are merely accidental by-products, why should we believe
them to be true? I see no reason for believing that one accident
would be able to give correct account of all the other accidents.[1]

A s you know by now, I am not an advocate of public (government)
education. I can't understand why Christians fight for the right to
recite or hear a prayer at a football game and yet have no problem expos-
ing their children to a curriculum that operates on the premise that God
does not exist. Then there is the never-ending battle over evolution, the
true established (false) religion of government education that tells students that they are cosmic accidents subsisting in a meaningless cosmos
without purpose or design. Am I exaggerating? Not according to evolutionist Richard Dawkins:

In the universe of blind physical forces and genetic replication, some people are going to get hurt, and other people are going to get lucky; and you won't find any rhyme or reason to it, nor any justice. The universe we observe has precisely the properties we should expect if there is at the bottom, no design, no purpose, no evil and no good. Nothing but blind pitiless indifference. DNA neither knows nor cares. DNA just is, and we dance to its music.[2]

Christians have been wasting their time, energy, and my money trying to get "equal time" for Intelligent Design (ID) to be taught in public schools when they could be getting a full-orbed biblically-based curriculum in a homeschool or institutional Christian school setting. These points were reinforced for me when Georgia State School Superintendent Kathy Cox wanted to deemphasize evolution in the science curriculum as a proven and uncontested scientific theory and allow for a discussion of "ID." She made the mistake of wanting to remove the word "evolution" and replace it with "biological changes over time." That would be like removing the word "Nazi" when telling the history of World War II.

Can Only Public-School Educated Kids do Science?

The *Atlanta-Journal Constitution* called Cox's anti-evolution position "irrational," a "sop to a handful of religious hard-liners who believe that schools should teach creationism, a belief born of faith rather than science." Just because a scientist believes that God created the cosmos does not mean that his abilities as a scientist are diminished. In fact, the case can be made that science got its start by people who believed God was the Creator of the cosmos and the laws that make it work and run consistently and predictably. They assumed that an experiment performed one day would have the same results, everything being equal, every day. In theory, an evolutionist could never make such an assumption since it's random changes, either minuscule or punctuated, that make evolution what it is.

History is on the side of Christians.[3] Robert Boyle (1627–1691), considered the "father of chemistry," was a devout Christian who, like Galileo, Johann Kepler (1571–1630), and Francis Bacon[4] (1561–1626) before him, challenged Aristotle's deductive approach to science in a much more consistent way. Boyle opposed the rationalists who believed that reason alone could produce sound and reliable science. Aristotle believed that the circle was the most perfect shape. He deduced from this that the orbits of the planets had to be circular, and the earth had to be the physical center of the cosmos because it was less than perfect in its appearance, unlike the heavenly bodies. Even the church fell for Aristotle's geocentric and spherical cosmology. Experimentation did not reveal the "truth" of geocentrism to Aristotle. He believed it because, to him, it made *logical* sense given his unfounded presuppositions.

Boyle rejected the Aristotelian "science" of his day and showed that a scientific theory should be "proved" by experimentation before considered as a law. The ordered consistency of the universe, created by God but showing the effects of the fall, led Boyle to adopt this view of science. In his last will and testament, Boyle "addressed his fellow members of the Royal Society of London, wishing them all success in 'their laudable attempts, to discover the true Nature of the Works of God' and 'praying that they and all other Searchers into Physical Truths' may thereby add 'to the glory of the Great Author of Nature, and to the Comforter of mankind.'"[5]

The title of one of Boyle's many books was *The Christian Virtuoso*, that is, "The Christian Scientist." Boyle was not a lone Christian voice crying in the wilderness of secular science. The membership of the Royal Society was made up of mostly Christians who shared Boyle's view that "the world was God's handiwork," and "it was their duty to study and understand this handiwork as a means of glorifying God."[6]

Evolutionary Slight of Hand

Boyle and other preeminent scientists of his day would have considered ID critics to be dishonest, irrational, and prejudicial. Anyone who sees a well-designed automobile assumes that it had a designer, even one found in a junk yard or partially disassembled in a scrap yard. Most people can tell the difference between the Grand Canyon and Mt. Rushmore without much thought. Anyone who decides to build a house calls in an architect. Every item that goes into building a car or a house was designed by someone with at least some intelligence. If a scientist, even one who received a Nobel Prize, tried to claim that there were no designers in building a microscope or telescope, he would be dismissed as a kook. But kids can be forced to believe that everything they see in the created order (nature), no matter how intricately put together, somehow evolved over time from some spontaneously generated primordial soup billions of years ago. Do we know this because someone saw it happen? Do we have evidence that one species evolved into another? Does the fossil record demonstrate macro- or even micro-evolutionary changes that resulted in new species? No. If scientists could demonstrate that evolution happened as they say it did, they would be the first to put the indisputable evidence on the table. They don't because they can't. It's one thing to prove that gravity exists, but it's another thing to prove *scientifically* (empirically) that an unknown evolutionary mechanism produced us.

Critics of ID don't realize how foolish they sound and how dependent on design theory they are in order to make evolution work. Consider Sharon Begley writing for *The Wall Street Journal*'s "Science Journal" section. In rejecting ID arguments to explain the origin of the universe, she trumpets the evolutionist's song: "Evolution could have co-opted them [proteins] when it was putting together the more complicated biochemical processes inside the animals, including people."[7] Evolution is not a thing, person, or even a force. It can't be seen, touched, or measured. As such, in terms of the elements science requires to be science; evolution as an entity does not exist. Following strict materialist presuppositions, evolution in and of itself cannot be studied. Even so, anti-IDers attribute personality, intelligence, design, and purpose to this miraculous phantasm they call "Evolution." A person "could have co-opted." A person could put something together, but "evolution" could not since it is not a thing; it's an idea. Evolution has become the new deity of the materialists with all the attributes of the God they so vehemently deny:

Before leaving this aspect of the Darwin story, it is worth noting that some among Darwin's staunchest supporters were far from being the materialistic rationalists they are sometimes painted. Even those who were not Christians used religious language to tell their story. For example, T. H. Huxley personalized "nature," referring to it as "fair, just and patient," "a strong angel who is playing for love. . . . A late as 1953 Julian Huxley conceded that his beliefs are "something in the nature of a religion." The distinguished biologist Lynn Margulis has rather scathingly referred to neo-Darwinism as "a minor twentieth century religious sect within the sprawling religious persuasion of Anglo-Saxon biology."[8]

Evolution is neither a person nor a force; it is a name for a myth that allows its propagators to get rid of God in the name of science. Like the Greek philosopher Epicurus (*c.* 341–271 B.C.), modern-day evolutionists don't want "a God who can derail our plans and mess up our day." Like Epicurus, evolutionists don't want a God "who is actively involved in the affairs of this world and who judges us in the next." To believe in such a God "is a surefire way to destroy one's personal peace and happiness."[9] This is why the facts don't matter to most evolutionists. They have a worldview to push, and it is manifesting itself in the divided court in Massachusetts mandating homosexual marriages and the mayor of San Francisco sanctioning homosexual marriages. "The motivation behind Darwinism today is its alternative moral and metaphysical vision rather than the promotion of science."[10] Darwinism "is theology masquerading as science."[11]

These are the hidden secrets. These are the facts that evolutionists don't want known. This is why they protect their monopoly with red meat ferocity. If word ever got out that the moral implications of evolution are harsh, cruel, and perverted, we might see a dramatic shift in support of the mythology parading as science. So in the meantime, it's necessary to hammer away at the absurdities of the evolutionary dogma.

Intellectual Ignorance

To demonstrate how out of touch critics of ID are, they paint Christians who believe that God designed and created the world as medieval obscurantists. The editors for the *Atlanta Journal-Constitution* write, "If faith replaces science as the standard in Georgia's classrooms, can we expect the banishment of globes from geography classes to placate flat-Earth folks? Would alchemy be given equal time with chemistry?" Even Jimmy Carter, who seems to be on the wrong side of so many issues, could not help attacking a straw man. "There is no need to teach," Carter stated in an Associated Press article, "that stars can fall out of the sky and land on a flat earth in order to defend our religious faith." Please tell me who in the ID or creation science community is teaching that the earth is flat, or even *has* taught that the earth is flat?

Carter and the editorial board at the *AJC* are as misinformed on history as they are on science. Washington Irving popularized the flat-earth myth in the nineteenth century when he published his three-volume biography on Christopher Columbus. Columbus did not battle the scientists and cartographers of his day over whether the earth was round or flat, as Irving claims, but over how big around the earth was. Belief in a round earth was an accepted scientific fact in the pre-enlightenment era. I suggest that Carter and the editors at the *AJC* read *Inventing the Flat Earth* by medieval scholar Dr. Jeffery Burton Russell, professor emeritus at the University of California, Santa Barbara, so they can see how their straw man arguments do not line up with the facts of history.

And what about alchemy? After reading so much pro-evolution literature, it seems to me that the evolutionists are the alchemists. They believe that highly organized and complex organic matter evolved from inorganic matter. To make things even more improbable, they have no way of accounting for the original matter that allows them to advance their irrational theories. Where did the super-dense proton that they claim contained the entire physical cosmos in the dark distant past before the spark of the "big bang" come from? And evolutionists claim that ID takes faith and is therefore outside the realm of science. Evolutionist Lynn E. Elfner claims he can "demonstrate evolution in a test tube." His first problem is accounting for the stuff that was used to make the test tube.[12]

Can Only Evolutionists Do Science?

The claim is made by many evolutionists, especially those who teach at the university level, that a person who does not believe in evolution cannot be a legitimate scientist. Carter implies this when he states, "As a Christian, a trained engineer and scientist, and a professor at Emory University [where he's not teaching science], I am embarrassed by Superintendent Kathy Cox's attempt to censor and distort education of Georgia's students."[13] Appealing to his academic training does not make him an authority on this issue. Carter hasn't done any real science since his Naval days.

Dr. Michael Behe, a respected professor of biochemistry, who also received a degree from Emory University and now teaches at Lehigh University, has pointed out numerous scientific and logical flaws in evolutionary reasoning in his book *Darwin's Black Box*. The point is, scientists disagree on the issue of origins based on their study of the evidence. The anti-intellectuals are those censors who control education by not allowing scientists like Behe to be heard in an academic setting. Evolutionists don't want the educational wards of the State to know that their theory has as much credibility as the blustering Wizard of Oz.

Propaganda Does Not Produce Followers

The claim is made by some that the reason creation arguments like those advanced by Behe are hard to refute is because the general public is not trained well enough in science. This is the argument of Steven Schafersman, who teaches biology, geology, and environmental science at the University of Texas of the Permian Basin in Odessa, Texas. He takes aim at creationists with this line of argument:

> We [evolutionists] recognize the absurdity of Behe's arguments because we understand logic and are trained in science, but that's 5% of the population. The success of creationism depends on the scientific illiteracy of the general citizenry, which is why creationists do so well. Sophistry, by definition, is convincing to listeners who don't realize it's sophistry.

The evolutionists have been in control of the public (government) schools in America for nearly a century. Evolution is promoted in movies (*Jurassic Park*, *The X-Men*, *March of the Penguins*), popular books (Carl Sagan's *Cosmos*,[14] *The Berenstain Bears*[15]), TV specials (PBS's *Dogs and More Dogs*), newspaper editorial pages, scientific journals (*Scientific American*), magazines (*National Geographic*), and museums. If the general population is not scientifically sophisticated enough to understand evolution, then the fault lies with the schools, and we must say with the evolutionists themselves since they control the science curriculum. With their near educational monopoly, the evolutionists have not been able to convince the majority of Americans of the validity of their theory. Many who are convinced don't understand evolution. This works to the evolutionists' favor. A letter writer to the *Atlanta Journal-Constitution*, in response to Georgia's evolution controversy, thinks "viruses . . . evolve." He considers this to be "proof" that evolution is true. Viruses may change, but no matter how much they change, they remain viruses. If evolution is simply change within a species, then we are all evolutionists. But change within a species is not enough to make evolution work. In order for evolution to be a theory with legs, a new species must emerge, not a variety of the original. Breeding dogs and cattle to enhance and perpetuate certain desirable characteristics is not evolution.

Public Relations Evolution

In order to get people to believe the "molecule to man" myth, evolutionists have created two forms of evolution: the Public Relations version which claims that God is involved in the evolutionary process and the hard-core atheist version that mandates that God does not exist. Equivocating on the meaning of the word "evolution" is the first step in eventually selling the hard-core version. Consider how Tim Berra, professor of zoology at Ohio State University, defines evolution:

> Everything evolves, in the sense of "descent with modification," whether it be government policy, religion, sports cars, or organisms. The revolutionary fiberglass Corvette evolved from more

mundane automotive ancestors in 1953. Other high points in the Corvette's evolutionary refinement included the 1962 model, in which the original 102-inch was shortened to 98 inches and the new closed-coupe Stingray model was introduced; the 1968 model, the forerunner of today's Corvette morphology, which emerged with removable roof panels; and the 1978 silver anniversary model, with fastback styling. Today's version continues the stepwise refinements that have been accumulating since 1953. The point is that the Corvette evolved through a selection process acting on variations that resulted in a series of transitional forms and an endpoint rather distinct from the starting point. A similar process shapes the evolution of organisms.[16]

Anyone with a modicum of common sense knows that the Corvette analogy is bogus. The first Corvette was designed by someone as was each new model. Evolution begins with the premise that there is no designer, and change is random, or as Richard Dawkins describes it, "blind." From initial conception to the first production model, the Corvette does not have a random item in it. There's nothing blind about it. The anti-Christian evolutionist and religious materialist Richard Dawkins is the epitome of irrationality and worldview blindness when he writes, "Biology is the study of complicated things that give the *appearance* of having been designed."[17] The evidence overwhelmingly discredits the evolutionary worldview, but Dawkins has a religion to defend. "This refusal to see what is before them . . . is what makes intelligent design theorists question whether there is something else motivating the materialist scientists with whom they debate, something that makes them resist the mounting scientific evidence for a designer."[18]

The Moral Problem

While there is still general skepticism about evolution by most Americans, there is also a great deal of ignorance. One letter writer to the *AJC* argues that since Darwin's *The Origin of Species* "implies no moral guidance, no idea of free will, no concept of the human spirit and eschatological basis," that such issues should be "addressed in the realms of religion and philosophy, which are not incompatible with scientific theory."[19] Here's the problem, at its root, Darwinism is atheistic. There is no religion; there is no god; and there are no morals. And that's just the way evolutionists want it.

Notes

1. C.S. Lewis, *God in the Dock* (Grand Rapids, MI: Eerdmans, 1970), 52–53.

2. Richard Dawkins, *River Out of Eden* (New York: HarperCollins, 1996), 133.

3. John Hudson Tiner, *For Those Who Dare: 101 Great Christians and How They Changed the World* (Green Forest, AR: Master Books, 2002).

4. For a discussion of Bacon's methodology, see Del Ratzsch, *Science and Its Limits: The Natural Sciences in Christian Perspective* (Downers Grove, IL: InterVarsity Press, 2000), 18–21.

5. Rodney Stark, *For the Glory of God: How Monotheism Led to Reformations, Science, Witch-Hunts, and the End of Slavery* (Princeton, NJ: Princeton University Press, 2003), 158.

6. Stark, *For the Glory of God*, 158.

7. Sharon Begley, "Evolution Critics Come Under Fire for Flaws in 'Intelligent Design,'" *The Wall Street Journal* (February 13, 2004), B1.

8. Philip J. Sampson, *6 Modern Myths about Christianity and Western Civilization* (Downers Grove, IL: InterVarsity Press, 2001), 62.

9. William A. Dembski, "Foreword," in Benjamin Wiker, *Moral Darwinism: How We Became Hedonists* (Downers Grove, IL: InterVarsity Press, 2002), 10.

10. Dembski, 11.

11. Dembski, 12.

12. Quoted in Marvin Olasky and John Perry, *Monkey Business: The True Story of the Scopes Trial* (Nashville, TN: Broadman & Holman, 2005), 208.

13. Quoted in Mary MacDonald, "Evolution furor heats up," *The Atlanta Journal-Constitution* (January 31, 2003), A1.

14. Carl Sagan, *Cosmos* (New York: Random House, 1980), 4.

15. Stan and Jan Berenstain, *The Berenstain Bears in The Bears' Nature Guide: A Nature Walk Through Bear Country* (New York: Random House, 1975), [6–7].

16. Tim Berra, *Evolution and the Myth of Creationism: A Basic Guide to the Facts in the Evolution Debate* (Stanford, CA: Stanford University Press, 1999), 118–119.

17. Richard Dawkins, *The Blind Watchmaker* (New York: Norton, 1986), 1. Emphasis added.

18. Wiker, *Moral Darwinism*, 21.

19. Shawn Buckley, Letter to the Editor, "Darwinists' evil agendas dishonor scientist," *The Atlanta Journal-Constitution* (February 14, 2004), A13

10

In The Name of Tolerance

[Herbert] Marcuse was a fashionable radical intellectual of the 1960s who believed that tolerance and free speech mostly serve the interests of the powerful. So he called frankly for "intolerance against movements from the right, and toleration of movements from the left." To restore the balance between oppressors and oppressed, he argued, indoctrination of students and "deeply pervasive" censorship of oppressors would be necessary, starting in college. By the late 1980s, many of the double standards Marcuse called for were in place.[1]

H OW DID CHRISTIANS lose formerly Christian institutions like Harvard, Yale, and Princeton to the humanists? The humanists never fired a shot. The take over came by way of a generous spirit of acceptance of less orthodox views in the name of tolerance. At its founding, Harvard required students to base their studies on the foundation of a comprehensive biblical worldview with Jesus Christ as the foundation. The directive was codified in 1636 in the following statement:

> Let every student be plainly instructed, and earnestly pressed to consider well, the main end of his life and studies is, *to know God and Jesus Christ which is eternal life*, John 17:3, and therefore

> to lay *Christ* in the bottom as the only foundation of all sound
> knowledge and learning. And seeing the Lord only giveth wis-
> dom, let every one seriously set himself by prayer in secret to
> seek it of him. Prov. 2, 3

Harvard remained steadfast in following the guidelines of this simple
but profound directive until the presidency of Increase Mather, who
served from 1685 to 1701. "His young colleagues regarded him as too
conservative, or unmovable, out of touch with their generation." Mather
was frequently absent from the school. He often traveled to England in
an attempt to secure the school's charter and that of the Bay Colony
itself. It was during his trips abroad that some began to promote "a new
spirit of innovation on the campus. The main instigators of this 'broad
and catholic [universal] spirit.'"[1]

The changes were not direct attacks on theology or morality. But
there was a call for an attitude of tolerance for differing opinions in areas where compromise did not seem to affect core issues. In time, there
was not only a breakdown in doctrinal beliefs but in morality as well.
Samuel Eliot Morison describes life at Harvard in the first quarter of the
eighteenth century in rather modern terms:

> It was an era of internal turbulence: for [President Benjamin]
> Wadsworth was no disciplinarian, and the young men resented
> a puritan restraint that was fast becoming obsolete. The facul-
> ty records, which begin with Wadsworth's administration, are
> full of "drinking frolicks," poultry-stealing, profane cursing and
> swearing, card-playing, live snakes in tutors' chambers, bring-
> ing "Rhum" into college rooms, and "shamefull and scandalous
> Routs and Noises for sundry nights in the College Yard."[2]

By 1805, Harvard had appointed Henry Ware, a Unitarian, to the Hollis
Chair of Divinity. Harvard was now lost. The tolerance door had been
opened in the spirit of fair play and an irenic spirit. But once the intrud-
ers had made their way through the door, the original Puritan orthodoxy would be shut out forever.

Since the slide into theological liberalism and moral libertinism was
gradual but methodological, those holding the minority and opposing

worldview were willing to bide their time as conservatives set the stage for their own self-destruction. Conservatives believed that "playing nice" and inviting the opposition to the party in terms of "dialog" and "civil discourse" would lead to acceptance and good will. Don't believe it; don't ever believe it!

Beware of Dialog

The latest trap is being set by those who want to dialog over the issue of homosexuality. Charles C. Haynes, senior scholar at the First Amendment Center in Arlington, Virginia, writes, "When it comes to homosexuality in public schools, we need not agree on what is right or wrong. But by bringing both sides of the issue into discussion, we can find peace."[3] Can you imagine what would have happened if this same approach had been taken with segregation or slavery? The anti-segregationists went into the battle with their feet firmly planted on the moral high ground. They weren't going to concede to the claim of moral neutrality. Their best weapon was their claim that segregation and slavery were unjust. Anything less and Blacks would still be sitting in the back of buses singing "we shall overcome."

Why doesn't Mr. Haynes adopt the same methodology and appeal to evolutionists to leave the dogmatism of their position out of the debate over origins as they engage in "civil discourse" with creationists? The Darwinists would have none of it. On this point, the Darwinists deserve credit. They defend their worldview against any and all opposition. They don't give an inch. If only Christians were so valiant, and, dare I say it, dogmatic.

There is only one goal that the pro-homosexual lobby wants to achieve—break down the resistance to the homosexual lifestyle without ever discussing what homosexuals actually do. It's obvious by the way rules for "civil discourse" are devised that the person with pre-conceived views on the immoral nature of homosexuality could not participate. Furthermore, there is no standard by which final moral decisions are to be made. In the end, all the two sides can agree on is to agree to disagree. Once this concession is made, the homosexuals have won.

A One-Way Street

For decades, religion in general and Christianity in particular have been expunged from public (government) schools in the name of the First Amendment. How many times have we heard the ACLU and Americans United for Separation of Church and State use the First Amendment to keep debates about religion and origins out of the schools? That's why it is disingenuous for Mr. Haynes to claim the following: "Religious liberty and freedom of expression are inalienable rights for all guaranteed by the First Amendment to the Constitution." The First Amendment is a one-way street. It is used to deny students with religious convictions the right to express themselves in the classroom. At the same time, the First Amendment is used to gain access to students who are cut off from parental authority and influence.

Once the public (government) schools have been homosexualized, the First Amendment will be used to exclude all opposition. The claim will be made that opposition to homosexuality is an "establishment of religion." Abstinence education is often denied because many who advocate it are operating from a religious point of view. The same is true of abortion and Intelligent Design. Let's not be fooled by "civil discourse" rhetoric; it's a wolf in sheep's clothing.

It's time that Christians set the guidelines by starting their own schools and establishing the ground rules for entry. Hopefully we've learned some lessons from what happened to Harvard, Yale, and Princeton.

Notes

1. David Beale, "The Rise and Fall of Harvard (1636–1805)," *Detroit Baptist Seminary Journal* (Fall 1998), 94.

2. Samuel Eliot Morison, *Three Centuries of Harvard: 1636–1936* (Cambridge: The Belknap Press of Harvard University Press, 1964), 78.

3. Charles C. Haynes, "A moral battleground, a civil discourse," *USA Today* (March 20, 2006), 15A.

My Genes Made Me Do It!

"Nature, Mr. Allnut, is what we are put in this world to rise above."[1]

I T USED TO be that education had a moral context and purpose. In fact, one of our nation's earliest documents, the Northwest Ordinance, passed by Congress on July 13, 1787, states, "Religion, morality, and knowledge, being necessary to good government and the happiness of mankind, schools and the means of education shall forever be encouraged."

> Fisher Ames, the framer of the wording of the First Amendment, stated, "Our liberty depends on our education, our laws, and habits . . . it is founded on morals and religion, whose authority reigns in the heart, and on the influence all these produce on public opinion before that opinion governs rulers."[2]

For years I have been collecting articles on genetic explanations for various abnormalities. Some are behavior related (eating too much), and some are disease related (prostate and breast cancer). In each case, however, the genetic cause is viewed as undesirable. Extraordinary measures and funding are recommended to fix the flaws. When scientists say they had discovered a "fat gene," "the finding was hailed by other researchers as pointing to a day when drugs might correct imbalances that cause some people to be hounded by food cravings and extra pounds while others remain lean."[3] If the cause of fatness is genetic, as homosexuals claim is true of their "orientation," then why the elation over the fat-gene discovery? If you're fat, it's not your fault. Anyone who proposes that a fat person should get thin, considering homosexual logic, is "fatophobic." Here are some other examples of gene-related conditions:

- "A genetic double-whammy rarely found in whites dramatically increases the risk of congestive heart failures in blacks."

- "Scientists say they have found a gene that predicts whether prostate cancer will develop into its most lethal form."

- "Researchers at McGill University in Montreal have discovered the gene that causes a devastating neurological disorder that is found almost exclusively among families along Quebec's North Shore."

- "A research team at two Mideast universities has developed a new way to genetically alter cells in living mice; offering new possibilities in the war against cancer and other diseases."[4]

- "Some of us, it seems, were just born to be bad. Scientists say they are on the verge of pinning down genetic and biochemical abnormalities that predispose their bearers to violence. An article in the journal *Science* . . . carried the headline EVIDENCE FOUND FOR POSSIBLE 'AGGRESSION' GENE."[5]

- "Apparently healthy men with normal weight and cholesterol levels are at three times higher risk of a heart attack if they have a common variation of a particular gene, researchers say."[6]

- "Salk Institute scientists say they have uncovered a gene that triggers certain forms of Leukemia, a discovery that may lead to the development of a screening test within the next few months."[7]

- "Researchers have found a brain chemical that boosts the craving for fat—and a way to block it without affecting the appetite for healthier foods."[8]

- "Why do gamblers often bet more after a losing hand? Or investors throw good money after bad? The answer may lie in the science of the brain."[9]

- "Is racism simply human nature or something learned from society? Neither, says a team of psychologists who, despite criticism, argue that racism represents an accidental side effect of evolution."[10]
- A recent article published in *The Sciences*, a New York Academy of Science magazine, stated that "rape is a 'natural, biological' phenomenon, springing from men's evolutionary urge to reproduce."[11]

Biological determinism rules the day. Of course, this is to be expected since every major university doing research has bought into the myth of Darwinism. How else can these bought-and-paid-for research scientists explain behavior? There are no conceptions of reality outside of biology. Sin? The fall of mankind? Self-government? Self-determination? What are these? All behavior *has* to be biological in origin given the underlying assumptions of evolution.

There's nothing new in any of this. Remnants of a theistic worldview have kept evolutionists from being truly consistent. The scientists who claim that rape is a "'natural, biological' phenomenon"[12] concede that "rapists are responsible for rape and should be punished." But why? How does the evolutionist account for morality given his materialistic presuppositions? Biological determinism makes people uncomfortable. They see it "as a threat to free will and personal responsibility, citing headlines like "MAN'S GENES MADE HIM KILL, HIS LAWYERS CLAIM. Behavioral geneticists are sometimes picketed, censored or compared with Nazis."[13]

This line of argument reminds me of a scene from the movie *The African Queen* (1951). Charlie Allnut (Humphrey Bogart) and Rose Sayer (Katherine Hepburn) are traveling down the very dangerous Ulanga River in Africa during World War I in an attempt to avoid capture by the Germans. Rose is a conservative Christian missionary and Charlie makes his living operating a mail boat hauling supplies. In contrast to Rose's character, Charlie is a bit more liberal who likes his gin a bit too much. After binging and passing out after one of his regular bouts with the bottle, Charlie wakes to see Rose pouring the contents of one of his precious gin bottles into the river. Charlie is visibly upset as he pleads with her: "Oh, Miss. Oh, have pity, Miss. You don't know what you're doing Miss. I'll perish without a hair of the dog. Oh, Miss, it ain't your property." Seeing that he's getting nowhere with this line of argument, he tries a kinder more subtle approach:

> Uh, how's the Book, Miss? [referring to the Bible]. Well, not that I ain't read it, that is to say, my poor old Mum used to read me stories out of it. How's about reading it out loud? I could sure do with a little spiritual comfort myself.

After getting the cold shoulder, Charlie lets his emotions fly and yells at her: "And you call yourself a Christian! Do you hear me? Don't ya? Don't ya? Huh?" She shows only a slight reaction but doesn't say a word. He backs up and goes about cleaning the relief valve on the boiler that's shaped like a cross—symbolic of the impact Rose is having on him and his circumstances. He asks for mercy: "What ya being so mean for, Miss? A man takes a drop too much once and a while; it's only human nature." Without looking up, she says the following: "Nature, Mr. Allnut, is what we are put in this world to rise above."

Penguins, Dog Vomit, Cannibalism, and Human Sexuality

And Tango Makes Three is an illustrated children's book about two male penguins that raise a baby penguin. It's based on a true story of two male penguins in New York City's Central Park Zoo that "adopt" a fertilized egg and raise the chick as their own. Some concerned parents see the book as a homosexual propaganda piece and want it removed from the library's regular shelves. A parent would have to consent before his or her child could check out the book. There's no doubt that the book is being pushed as a homosexual primer to soften up young minds for the more scholarly propaganda. In *Biological Exuberance*, for example, author Bruce Bagemihl claims, "The world is, indeed, teeming with homosexual, bisexual and transgendered creatures of every stripe and feather. . . . From the Southeastern Blueberry Bee of the United States to more than 130 different bird species worldwide, the 'birds and the bees,' literally, are queer."[14]

Here's the premise: Whatever animals do in nature is natural. What's natural is normal. What's normal is moral. So if penguins engage in homosexual behavior, then that behavior must be natural, normal, and moral. How can we mere mortals impose our rules of sexual behavior on what's natural in the animal kingdom? Homosexuals extrapolate that what animals do naturally in nature applies to what higher animals can do naturally without judgment. But the lower animal/higher animal model breaks down when other so-called natural behaviors in animals are considered. For example, the Bible states, "It has happened to them according to the true proverb, 'A DOG RETURNS TO ITS OWN VOMIT' [Prov. 26:11] and, 'A sow, after washing, returns to wallowing in the mire'" (2 Pet. 2:22). Now I would like to see the homosexual propagandists explain how these behaviors might explain the normality of animal behavior and its human parallels.

Consider the case of Timothy Treadwell depicted in the movie *Grizzly Man*. He lived among bears for 13 years and thought of them as his "family." In 2003, Treadwell and his companion, Amie Huguenard, were mauled and mostly eaten by one of the Alaskan grizzly bears he considered to be part of his extended animal family. While he thought of the bears as his brothers and sisters, the bears thought of him as lunch. Then there's the case of Armin Meiwes who killed and ate 43-year-old Bernd-Jurgen Brandes.[15] What did Mr. Meiwes do that was wrong given the premise that animal behavior is a normative model for human behavior?[16]

A few years ago, I saw an advertisement for a television special on Turner Network Television—"The Trials of Life." The full-page advertisement showed a composite picture of six animals, one of which was the bald eagle, with the following caption: "Discover how similar the face of nature is to yours. The way you love, the way you fight, the way you grow, all have their roots in the kingdom we all live in: the animal kingdom." The implication here is obvious: Humans are only an evolutionary step away from *other* animals. In biblical terms, men and women are not animals. God did not create Adam out of another pre-existing animal.

While channel surfing, I came across the second installment of the six-part series of "The Trials of Life." I soon learned what Benjamin Franklin meant when he described the eagle as a bird of "bad moral character." With two eaglets in the nest and not enough food to go around, mamma allows the weakest eaglet to die. She then cannibalizes the dead eaglet and feeds it to the survivor. Was this natural or unnatural? Is this moral animal behavior that we should emulate? How do we know? Should we follow the example of the eagles or just the homosexual penguins?

We mustn't forget other "natural" animal behaviors. Animals rape on a regular basis. Should we make the leap the homosexuals want to make regarding penguins? If homosexual behavior in penguins is a template for human sexuality, then why can't a similar case be made for rape among humans? As hard as it might be to believe, the connection has been made. Randy Thornhill, a biologist, and Craig T. Palmer, an anthropologist, attempt to demonstrate in their book *A Natural History of Rape*[17] that evolutionary principles explain rape as a "genetically developed strategy sustained over generations of human life because it is a kind of sexual selection—a successful reproductive strategy." They go on to claim, however, that even though rape can be explained genetically in evolutionary terms, this does not make the behavior morally right. Of course, given Darwinian assumptions, there is no way to condemn rape on moral grounds. The same could be said for homosexual behavior, and everything else. If we are truly the products of evolution, then there can be no moral judgments about anything. So then, if the homosexuals want to use penguins as their moral model, then they need to take all animal behavior into consideration when they build their moral worldview. If we should follow the animal world regarding homosexual penguins and thereby regard human homosexual behavior as normal, then we must be consistent and follow the animal world regarding rape, eating our young, and eating our neighbors decriminalize these behaviors as well.

Without an appeal to a fixed moral standard that is above nature, there is no way to criticize "barnyard morality." Public schools have no place to go to develop a moral worldview that won't get them in trouble with the ACLU and the secular courts.

Notes

1. From *The African Queen* (1951).

2. Fisher Ames, *An Oration on the Sublime Virtues of General George Washington* (Boston: Young & Minns, 1800), 23.

3. Jeff Nesmith, "Dieters' dream: Gene to control fat found," *Atlanta Constitution* (December 1, 1994), C1.

4. These four examples were taken from the "Science News" section of the *Atlanta Journal-Constitution* (October 10, 2002), A9.

5. Dennis Overbye, "Born to Raise Hell?," *Time* (February 21, 1994), 76.

6. Amanda Huted, "Gene variant could mean higher risk of heart attack," *Atlanta Journal/Constitution* (October 15, 1992), C3.

7. "Gene discovery could lead to leukemia screening test," *Atlanta Journal/ Constitution* (October 3, 1992), E8.

8. Tim Friend, "Brain chemical may feed craving for fat," *USA Today* (October 29, 1992), 1A.

9. Faye Flam, "Study: Reckless gambler, blame your brain," *The Atlanta Journal-Constitution* (March 22, 2002), A18.

10. Dan Vergano, "Racism may have evolutionary link," *USA Today* (December 11, 2001), 11.

11. Dan Vergano, "'Natural, biological' theory of rape creates instant storm," *USA Today* (January 28, 2000), 8D.

12. Vergano, "'Natural, biological' theory of rape creates instant storm," 8D.

13. Steven Pinker, "Are Your Genes to Blame?," *Time* (January 20, 2003), 99.

14. Cristina Cardoze, "They're in love. They're gay. They're penguins. . . . And they're not alone" (June 6, 2006): http://www.jrn.columbia.edu/studentwork/cns/2002-06-10/591.asp.

15. http://news.bbc.co.uk/2/hi/europe/3286721.stm

16. Theodore Dalrymple, "The Case for Cannibalism" (January 5, 2005): http://www.city-journal.org/html/eon_01_05_04td.html

17. Randy Thornhill and Craig T. Palmer, *A Natural History of Rape: Biological Bases of Sexual Coercion* (Cambridge, MA: MIT Press, 2000).

Part III

12

Turning Away From Myths

For the time will come when they will not endure sound doctrine;
but wanting to have their ears tickled, they will accumulate for
themselves teachers in accordance to their own desires, and will
turn away their ears from the truth and will turn aside to myths"
(2 Tim. 4:1–4).

OURS IS AN era when myths, legends, hoaxes,[1] and conspiracies abound. Much of the dubious credit for this phenomenon is probably the result of the ever-present Internet. Mythological concoctions travel at the speed of light and find their way to open email inboxes where unsuspecting and gullible readers embrace them as the gospel truth. Alex Boese, author of *The Museum of Hoaxes*, writes that "Deception surrounds us everywhere: on TV, on the radio, in newspapers, and on the Internet. In its brief existence the Internet has become the great incubator of every lie, rumor, and half-baked idea imaginable. Internet message boards brim over with slanders and false allegations."[2] But as he later demonstrates with a long history of examples, there is nothing new in pulling the wool over the eyes of the gullible. It's been going on for a long time. In fact, the more unbelievable a story is, it seems the more people want to believe it. In an odd sort of way, for some people believing the absurd, to borrow Tertullian's (*c.* 160–225) often quoted but often misunderstood statement,[3] is thought to be the pathway to true faith and knowledge.

The post-enlightenment era with its emphasis on reason and neutral facts was not the hoped for antidote. The academic disciplines are not immune to buying into or perpetuating myths, legends, and hoaxes—everything from the flat-earth tale perpetuated by Washington Irving in his three-volume *History of the Life and Voyages of Christopher Columbus* [4] and claims that the "Piltdown Man" was an evolutionary missing link to the insistence by some that the Moon landings had been staged[5] and that 9–11 was a government conspiracy.[6]

Charles Babbage (1791–1871), an English scientist and mathematician who conceptualized the idea of a programmable computer, understood that even scientists were often guilty of manipulating evidence to add credibility to a theory. He described three types of misconduct: forging, trimming, and cooking:

> Forging was the outright invention of data, and was thankfully rare. Trimming was the cosmetic 'massaging' of data, so as to display them to best advantage; . . . Cooking meant discretely losing the data that were out of line or did not help the hypothesis. . . . Trimming and cooking are not so uncommon, and they merge at one extreme into the exercise of judgment and experience. They almost invariably accompany an inner certainty on the part of the scientist that his conclusions are correct and scarcely need yet more evidence.[7]

A careful and practiced eye will be on the alert for attempts to manipulate the evidence to support a preconception of a theory.

Historical and Scientific Frauds

We generally hold on to the myth that the scientific community is somehow unaffected from propagating and disseminating falsehoods. To this day some evolutionists continue to push the faked embryo drawings[8] of German biologist Ernst Haeckel (1834–1919), even after they had been exposed as fraudulent as early as 1868 and some of his other deceptions were exposed in the book *Haeckel's Frauds and Forgeries.*[9] Modern textbooks continue to include his "ontogeny recapitulates phylogeny" drawings as proof of evolution. For example, in 2004 they "were used as evidence for Darwinism in the tenth edition of Starr and Taggart's *Biology: Patterns and Processes of Life*; and in the third edition of Voet and Voet's *Biochemistry*."[10] Once in the historical pipeline, these "myth-stories" have been difficult to flush out of the historical pipeline that runs through the educational establishment.

Consider the debate between Thomas Henry Huxley and Samuel Wilberforce (1805–1873), the Bishop of Oxford, on the credibility of Charles Darwin's thesis as presented in the 1859 publication of *On the Origin of Species.* The debate took place during the June 30, 1860 meeting of the British Association at Oxford. The following description of the debate appears "in *every* distinguished biography of Darwin and of Huxley, as well as in every popular history of the theory of evolution."[11] Here's the often cited description of what supposedly transpired at the debate:

> I was happy enough to be present on the memorable occasion at Oxford when Mr Huxley bearded Bishop Wilberforce. . . . . [T]he Bishop rose, and in a light scoffing tone, florid and fluid, he assured us there was nothing in the idea of evolution. Then, turning to his antagonist with a smiling insolence, he begged to know, was it through his grandfather or his grandmother that he claimed his descent from a monkey? On this Mr Huxley slowly and deliberately arose. A slight tall figure stern and pale, very quiet and very grave, he stood before us, and spoke those tremendous words—words which no one seems sure of now, nor I think, could remember just after they were spoken, for their meaning took away our breath, though it left us in no doubt as to what it was. He was not ashamed to have a monkey for his ancestor; but he would be ashamed to be connected with a man who used great gifts to obscure the truth. No one doubted his meaning and the effect was tremendous.[12]

This "eye-witness" reporting of the debate first appeared in the October 1898 issue of *Macmillan's Magazine*, in an article entitled "A Grandmother's Tales," nearly forty years after the event! No other account of the Huxley-Wilberforce debate "mentioned remarks concerning Huxley's monkey ancestors or claimed that he made a fool of the bishop. To the contrary, many thought the bishop had the better of it, and even many of the committed Darwinians thought it at most a draw."[13]

So why does the above unsubstantiated account of the debate persist? J.R. Lucas offers the following explanation: "[T]he quarrel between religion and science came not because of what Wilberforce said, but because it was what Huxley wanted; and as Darwin's theory gained supporters, they took over his view of the incident,"[14] this in spite of the fact that Darwin's own correspondence states that he saw merit in a number of Wilberforce's arguments that had been published in an earlier review of *On the Origin of Species*. Darwin wrote, "'By the way, the Bishop makes a very telling case against me.' Indeed, several of Wilberforce's comments caused Darwin to make modifications in a later revision of the book."[15] The manufactured scene is used as propaganda, a tool to disparage any critic who dares to point out the myth behind the message.

Paying for Results

Careers, reputations, the desire for tenure, and government funding often are behind the perpetuation of myths as scientific fact. In his January 17, 1961 Farewell Address, President Dwight D. Eisenhower described how government grants might get in the way of what should be objective scientific research and discovery:

> The prospects of domination of the nation's scholars by federal employment, project allocations, and the power of money is ever present—and is gravely to be regarded. Yet, holding scientific research and discovery in respect, we would, we must always be alert to the equal and opposite danger that public policy could itself become a captive of a scientific-technological elite.[16]

To get to the point, some people, scientists included, will do almost anything for money, power, and prestige—even lie! To put it more kindly, "like other people, scientists are interested in seeing their projects flourish, and their enthusiasm can blind them to the possible negative effects of their work."[17]

Some of the world's greatest scientists are not above fudging research findings.[188] One author goes so far as to describe some scientific claims as "bad and bogus."[19] David Stove, who is himself an evolutionist, calls a number of Darwinian arguments in defense of the position "fairytales" and "fables."[20] A high price is sometimes paid by scientific myth busters. When Dr. Peter Duesberg, a professor of molecular and cell biology at the University of California-Berkeley, suggested "that HIV might not be the cause of AIDS and that AIDS might be nothing more than a collection of diseases diagnosed as AIDS when HIV was present," he "was transformed into a scientific leper, his arguments never receiving serious consideration."[21] According to Ghislaine Lanctôt (pronounced "Ghee-Lane Lank-Toe"), a French-Canadian medical doctor and author of the book *Medical Mafia: How to Get Out of It Alive and Take Back Our Health and Wealth*, there are repercussions to taking the road less traveled, that is, the road not paved with government grants:

> Sticks are used to beat you up for not following the herd. Disobedient people are the ones who don't serve big money. The first stick is the "stick of exclusion." You'll be fired. That stops 95 percent of the people from speaking up.
>
> The second stick is the "stick of dispossession." You'll have your title taken away. You'll have your right of titles taken away. You'll have your prestige taken away. You'll be put down. Your money will be taken away. Your house, your car . . . anything that will make you shut up.
>
> If that is not enough, then the third stick is the "stick of elimination." You'll be put in jail or a mental institution. . . . The question is, "Are you going to be afraid of the sticks?"[22]

There is a fourth stick. If you don't agree with the party line going in, you'll never get hired in the first place. No one likes a trouble maker, especially when government money is at stake.

No Christian Immunity

Christians are not immune to uncorroborated stories that are passed along as fact. To this day, reports that "famed atheist Madalyn Murray O'Hair is petitioning the federal government to ban all religious broadcasting"[23] still abound, even though she died in 1995.[24]

The hardest myths to dispel are those that are based on some perceived unimpeachable authority,[25] whether science or Scripture. If we are told that the Bible teaches something in regard to history or theology, then we should believe it. In fact, as Christians, we would defend the Bible against all claims to the contrary. But if the Bible does not teach what some claim it teaches, then we should reject these false assertions for what they really are—*myths* (2 Peter 1:16; Titus 1:14; 1 Tim. 1:4; 4:7).

We must be careful not to go where the Bible does not go and defend things the Bible never discusses. A biblical worldview does not mean that everything we know can only be derived from the words of the Bible. The study of God's creation is a noble and worthwhile enterprise. We should not be afraid of what we might discover as we look through a microscope to view the smallest and nearest things of God's creation or as we gaze through a telescope to see the largest and most distant elements of the cosmos created and held together by God's sovereign power (Col. 1:16–17; Heb. 1:2). In fact, every new discovery enhances the truthfulness of Scripture even though materialists might try to claim otherwise. If we are commanded to "test the spirits to see whether they are from God" (1 John 4:1), then it would behoove all of us to test the claims of secularists and saints alike to see whether they conform as well (Acts 17:11). Not everything a Christian says on every point of knowledge is biblical. Just because someone claims divine authority or proclaims "Thus says the Lord," does not make him a carrier of truth. Let's not be so quick to believe in things that might tickle our ears. Discernment takes practice (Heb. 5:14).

Notes

1. Geoff Tiballs, *The World's Greatest Hoaxes: The Exploits of Ingenious Hoaxers, Cunning Imposters, and their Gullible Victims* (New York: Barnes and Noble, 2006).

2. Alex Boese, *The Museum of Hoaxes: A Collection of Pranks, Stunts, Deceptions, and Other Wonderful Stories Contrived for the Public from the Middle Ages to the New Millennium* (New York: Dutton, 2002), 1.

3. "I believe because it is absurd." (*De Carne Christi* [5.4]).

4. Jeffrey Burton Russell, *Inventing the Flat Earth: Columbus and Modern Historians* (New York: Praeger, 1991). Also see Thomas E. Woods, Jr., "The Flat Earth Myths": www.lewrockwell.com/woods/woods46.html

5. Marcia Dunn, "Moon Hoax claims hard to stomp out," *The Atlanta Journal-Constitution* (December 26, 2002), A6.

6. David Ray Griffin, *Christian Faith and the Truth Behind 9/11: A Call to Reflection and Action* (Louisville, KY: Westminster John Knox Press, 2006). For a response to Griffin's claims, see http://mu-warrior.blogspot.com/2006/08/official-presbyterian-publisher-issues.html and the "Fact Sheet" from The National Institute of Standards and Technology: http://wtc.nist.gov/pubs/factsheets/faqs_8_2006.htm

7. Walter Gratzer, *The Undergrowth of Science: Delusion, Self-Deception and Human Frailty* (Oxford, New York: Oxford University Press, 2000), vii.

8. http://wnd.com/images/evolvedrawing.jpg

9. J. Assmusth and Ernest R. Hull, *Haeckel's Frauds and Forgeries* (India: Bombay Press, 1911). Even pro-evolutionary biographies on Haeckel admit that some of his research had been "discredited" but still had "shaped scientific thought of the period, including the psychoanalytic theories of Sigmund Freud." Haeckel is described as "often reckless in his methods, as if he had some kind of direct line to the source of evolutionary truth." (Richard Milner, "Haeckel, Ernst [1834–1919]," *The Encyclopedia of Evolution: Humanity's Search for Its Origins* (New York: Facts on File, 1990], 206).

10. Jonathan Wells, *The Politically Incorrect Guide to Darwinism and Intelligent Design* (Washington, D.C.: Regnery Publishing, Inc., 2006), 28. Also see Jonathan Wells, *Icons of Evolution: Science or Myth?* (Washington, D.C.: Regnery Publishing, Inc., 2000).

11. Rodney Stark, *For the Glory of God: How Monotheism Led to Reformations, Science, Witch-Hunts, and the End of Slavery* (Princeton, NJ: Princeton University Press, 2003), 188.

12. Isabella Sidgwick, "A Grandmother's Tales," *Macmillan's Magazine*, 78:468 (October 1898), 433–434. Cited in J.R. Lucas, "Wilberforce and Huxley: A Legendary Encounter" (1979): http://users.ox.ac.uk/~jrlucas/legend.html#r-3

13. Stark, *For the Glory of God*, 188.

14. J.R. Lucas, "Wilberforce and Huxley." Quoted in Stark, *For the Glory of God*, 189.

15. Stark, *For the Glory of God*, 189.

16. Quoted in Patrick J. Michaels, *Meltdown: The Predictable Distortion of Global Warming by Scientists, Politicians, and the Media* (Washington, D.C.: Cato Institute, 2004), vii.

17. Ruth Hubbard and Elijah Wald, *Exploring the Gene Myth: How Genetic Information Is Produced and Manipulated by Scientists, Physicians, Employers, Insurance Companies, Educators, and Law Enforcers* (Boston: Beacon Press, 1993), xiii.

18. Alexander Kohn, *False Prophets: Fraud and Error in Science and Medicine* (New York: Basil Blackwell), 1988. When Dr. Peter Duesberg, a professor of molecular and cell biology at the University of California-Berkeley suggested "that HIV might not be the cause of AIDS and that AIDS might be nothing more than a collection of diseases diagnosed as AIDS when HIV was present," he "was transformed into a scientific leper, his arguments never receiving serious consideration." (Morris E. Chafetz, *Big Fat Liars: How Politicians, Corporations, and the Media Use Science and Statistics to Manipulate the Public* [Nashville, TN: Nelson Current, 2005], 46).

19. Martin Gardner, *Good, Bad and Bogus* (Buffalo, NY: Prometheus Books, 1981).

20. David Stove, *Darwinian Fairytales: Selfish Genes, Errors of Heredity, and Other Fables of Evolution* (New York: Encounter Books, 2006).

21. Chafetz, *Big Fat Liars*, 46.

22. Quoted in Joseph Mercola, *The Great Bird Flu Hoax* (Nashville, TN: Thomas Nelson, 2006), 44.

23. Doug Trouten, "Attack of the Fifty-Foot Hoax," *Charisma* (April 1998), 68. For a detailed history of the supposed FCC ban, go to http://www.snopes.com/politics/religion/fcc.asp

24. The petition is cited as RM-2493. The petition still circulates, usually misspelling O'Hair as "O'Hare."

25. David Murray, Joel Schwartz, and S. Robert Lichter, *It Ain't Necessarily So: How Media Make and Unmake the Scientific Picture of Reality* (New York: Roman & Littlefield Publishers, 2001).

They Never Said It

"History will be kind to me, for I intend to write it."[1]

THE WINNERS OF any contest, whether intellectual, political, or military, work very hard to formulate the history of the conflict so their side of the story is told in the best possible light. As one might expect, there is a great deal of bias in the way history is reported. In order to put the historical accounting in the best possible light for those who are reading the history for the first time, sometimes the facts are manipulated just enough to reinforce the impression that the right side did indeed win the contest and left the opposition in the dust. There are some cases where contrary facts are never brought into the discussion so as not to raise questions and doubts in the minds of readers that there might have been a good reason why there was a debate and a battle in the first place. And it isn't beyond some historians to manufacture their own versions of historical events and then hope that no one notices or checks the original sources.

The Myth of Objectivity

Facts are never neutral, and they do not speak for themselves.[2] Facts are lined up in defense of a position and then interpreted. Some facts never make it to the interpreter's table. Too many people believe that newscasters, journalists, and scientists simply "report the facts" devoid of biases, preconceived assumptions, or political agendas. This is hardly the case as James Davison Hunter points out in his book *Culture Wars*:

> In the very act of *selecting* the stories to cover, the books to pub-
> lish and review, the film and music to air, and the art to exhibit,
> these institutions effectively define what topics are important
> and which issues are relevant—worthy of public consideration.
> Moreover, in the *substance* of the stories covered, books pub-
> lished and reviewed, art exhibited, and so on, the mass media act
> as a filter through which our perceptions of the world around us
> take shape. Thus, by virtue of the decisions made by those who
> control the mass media—seemingly innocuous decisions made
> day to day and year to year—those who work within these insti-
> tutions cumulatively wield enormous power.[3]

The fact that a story even gets on a thirty-minute news slot should make all of us question the notion of neutrality in reporting or in anything else. There is no such thing as pure, unfiltered, pristine news or history. All news and historical accounting carries a bias, whether liberal or conservative; it's the result of how we want the world to be seen.[4] Of course, the way *we* see the world is the right way to see the world. Anyone who sees the world in a different way is seeing it the wrong way. "Network anchor David Brinkley once admitted, 'News is what I say it is—it's something worth knowing by *my* standards!'"[5] Knowing this helps to remove the interpretive blinders from our own eyes.

William Proctor, a veteran reporter and author who has worked for the New York *Daily News*, explains that the "[media] gospel is rooted in a kind of secular theology that purports to convey infallible social, moral, and political truth—a truth that the paper [*The New York Times*] fervently promotes with all the zeal of the fieriest proselytizer."[6] Proctor describes the editorial and news-gathering policy at the *Times* as "Man-hattan Fundamentalism," "a well-defined but also rather rigid package of viewpoints which the paper disseminates widely to influence political, social, and personal beliefs and behaviors."[7] Even the choice of a story shows bias. Marvin Olasky writes: "Since only an omniscient God can be truly objective, man's 'objectivity' is inherently biased, TIME staffers, recognizing that, increasingly emphasize subjectivity, but that's no solution either."[8]

In 1986, Robert Bazell of NBC, admitted that "Objectivity is a fallacy. . . . There are different opinions, but you don't have to give them equal weight." Linda Ellerbee wrote that "There is no such thing as objectivity. Any reporter who tells you he's objective is lying to you."[9]

It's Not Just the Media

The coldly objective, rationalistic, and materialistic field of science claims to be immune from presuppositional bias. At least that's what scientists want non-scientists like us to believe. Science is not an objective field of study, and it doesn't operate independent of certain non-empirical starting assumptions, as Paul Davies, Professor of Mathematical Physics, points out:

> However successful our scientific explanations may be, they always have certain starting assumptions built in. For example, an explanation of some phenomenon in terms of physics presupposes the validity of the laws of physics, which are taken as given. But one may ask where these laws come from in the first place. One could even question the origin of logic upon which all scientific reasoning is founded. Sooner or later we all have to accept something as given, whether it's God, or logic, or a set of laws, or some other foundation for existence. Thus "ultimate" questions will always lie beyond the scope of empirical science as it is usually defined.[10]

Beyond these "ultimate" questions, there are certain presuppositions that prevail among materialist philosophers and scientists that color the facts. How is it possible to reason with Lawrence Lerner, professor emeritus at California State University in Long Beach, when he claims, "There are no alternatives to evolution that are science," and that all the "alternatives are religious"?[11] Any piece of evidence that is put forth that might contradict the evolutionary model will be dismissed out of hand as non-factual, creating an interpretive "Catch-22." At the same time, Lerner and other evolutionists will claim that they are being scientifically objective when *they* evaluate the facts. Even the late evolutionist Stephen Jay Gould admitted that scientists have their own set of biases that they bring to a study of the facts: "The stereotype of a fully rational and objective 'scientific method,' with individual scientists as logical (and interchangeable) robots, is self-serving mythology."[12] Objectivity and neutrality, as they relate to the defense of one's worldview, are myths.

> Beware of the man who tells you that he will explain—fully explain—any complex human action or event by resorting to "coldly objective," "empirically verifiable," "statistical data." He is deceiving himself, and perhaps seeking to deceive you.
> For in the first place we do not all see the same event in exactly the same way, let alone interpret it the same way—not even events which do not involve the complicating factor of human purpose.[13]

While the study of the facts of history is of the utmost importance, we must never forget that someone is always choosing what facts will go into textbooks and how they should be interpreted. To be forewarned is to be forearmed.

Sloppy Scholarship

Sloppy scholarship also plays a role in fractured historical accounts as one writer quotes another writer without realizing that the first writer never based his study on original source documents for support of his historical claims. The quotation or referenced event is repeated so often by so many in any number of authoritative sources that it *must* be true. Conservatives as well as liberals perpetuate historical myths so as to lend historical credibility to their respective causes. It's unfortunate that those who are duped by historic myth-telling are the ones who genuinely want to know the truth and are trusting of those who put their views in print. As I hope to show, it's this willingness to trust what's in print that has led to the distorted history of the relationship between religion, science, and history that has made its way into textbooks. Not even Christians are immune.

Will the Real James Madison Please Stand Up?

For years Christian writers have attributed the following quotation to James Madison (1751–1836), the Princeton-educated fourth president of the United States, in hopes of supporting the often repeated claim that the Ten Commandments served as the foundational law system of the early colonial constitutions, judicial codes, and Federal Constitution:

> We have staked the whole future of American Civilization, not upon the power of government, far from it. We have staked the future of all of our political institutions upon the capacity of each of us to govern ourselves, to control ourselves, to sustain ourselves according to the Ten Commandments of God.[14]

While this is a great statement that can be supported without Madison's endorsement,[15] no one has been able to locate the original source documentation that would unequivocally tie the statement to him. My investigation led only as far back as the January 1958 issue of *Progressive Calvinism* where the source of the quotation is a 1958 calendar published by Spiritual Mobilization. What was Spiritual Mobilization's source for the quotation? We're not told.

There is another *possible* origin for the quotation. *Bishop* James Madison (1749–1812), a cousin of President Madison, served as president of William and Mary College and was the first Protestant Episcopal bishop of Virginia. It was *this* James Madison who said, "Good morals can spring only from the bosom of religion."[16] It would not be difficult to confuse the two Madisons. In fact, in naming what is now James Madison University, "The *Daily News-Record* columnist wasn't even convinced that Madison College honored President James Madison. 'It is claimed by some,' the columnist wrote, 'that those who suggested Madison as the new name did not have the president in mind, but Bishop James Madison.'"[17] Even so, there is no tangible evidence that even this James Madison said it. Until someone actually finds unimpeachable evidence to the contrary, the statement as attributed to *President* James Madison or *Bishop* James Madison must be regarded as a fabrication.

He Never Said It

Then there's the attribution of the following citation to historian Alexander Fraser Tytler (or Tyler) (1747–1813). While it supports what many believe are important political observations about the rise and fall of natons, is it authentic?:

> A democracy is always temporary in nature; it simply cannot exist as a permanent form of government. A democracy will continue to exist up until the time that voters discover that they can vote themselves generous gifts from the public treasury. From that moment on, the majority always votes for the candidates who promise the most benefits from the public treasury, with the result that every democracy will finally collapse due to loose fiscal policy, which is always followed by a dictatorship.
>
> The average age of the world's greatest civilizations from the beginning of history, has been about 200 years. During those 200 years, these nations always progressed through the following sequence:
> From Bondage to spiritual faith;
> From spiritual faith to great courage;
> From courage to liberty;
> From liberty to abundance;
> From abundance to complacency;
> From complacency to apathy;
> From apathy to dependence;
> From dependence back into bondage.

Like the dubious James Madison quotation, the Tytler extract is cited on a regular basis and often finds its way into published works.[18] While there was an Alexander Tytler, there is no extant evidence that puts these words in his mouth or in any of his published works. Supposedly it can be found in a book written by Tytler that goes by the title *The Fall of the Athenian Republic* or *The Decline and Fall of the Athenian Republic*. There is no such book in circulation or attributed to him. Others claim that the quotation can be located in Tytler's *Elements of General History: Ancient and Modern*, a book that does exist. The following response from the library of the University of Edinburgh states that their research has shown that the quotation does not appear in the library's holdings of Tytler's books:

> Edinburgh University Library occasionally receives enquiries, particularly from North America, about this particular work. However, this title is not in our Library holdings, nor does it appear in the stocks of the other major research libraries in the United Kingdom. . . . Locally, the chapters of Tytler's *General History* . . . (which we DO have) has been checked on the off-chance that *The Decline and Fall [of the Athenian Republic]* might have been a chapter title . . . but it is not. . . . We have scanned our holdings pretty thoroughly on different occasions, going back a few years now, but we have not found the quotation or anything similar to it, but we cannot absolutely rule out the possibility that we have missed it.[19]

Even the United States Library of Congress has been called in on the search with no success in finding the much cited but questionable quotation. Even so, the Madison and Tytler quotations continue to circulate as authentic history. Here's the lesson to be learned: If there are so many who are willing to accept the authenticity of historical citations with something less than a shred of evidence, then it shouldn't surprise us when students accept historical accounts found in textbooks and scholarly journals that have about the same amount of evidentiary support. The difference, however, is that so much of what finds its way into textbooks and popular works of history affect the way Christianity and the Bible are portrayed. It's one thing to be wrong about a few unsupported quotations; it's another thing to reshape a school curriculum based on fabricated history that relegates the Bible to the dust bin of history.

Notes

1. Attributed to Winston Churchill (1874–1965).

2. Roy A. Clouser, *The Myth of Religious Neutrality: An Essay on the Hidden Role of Religious Belief in Theories* (Notre Dame, IN: University of Notre Dame Press, 1991), 26–27.

3. James Davison Hunter, *Culture Wars: The Struggle to Define America* (New York: Basic Books, 1991), 225.

4. Bernard Goldberg, *Bias: CBS Insider Exposes How the Media Distort the News* (Washington, D.C.: Regnery, 2002), 5.

5. David Brinkley, quoted by Edith Efron, "Why Speech on Television Is Not Really Free," *TV Guide* (April 11, 1964), 7. Quoted in Colleen Cook, *All That Glitters: A News-Person Explores the World of Television* (Chicago: Moody Press, 1992), 32.

6. William Proctor, *The Gospel According to the New York Times: How the World's Most Powerful News Organization Shapes Your Mind and Values* (Nashville, TN: Broadman & Holman, 2000), 11–12

7. Proctor, *The Gospel According to the New York Times*, 31.

8. Marvin Olasky, "Progress Report: A Changing WORLD amid a subjective TIME," *World* (October 14, 2006), 40.

9. Dinesh D'Souza, "Mr. Donaldson Goes to Washington," *Policy Review* (Summer 1986), 24–31. Quoted in Marvin Olasky, *Prodigal Press: The Anti-Christian Bias of the American News Media* (Westchester, IL: Crossway Books, 1988), 59.

10. Paul Davies, *The Mind of God: The Scientific Basis for a Rational World* (New York: Simon & Schuster, 1992), 15.

11. Mary MacDonald, "A textbook case in Cobb County," *Atlanta-Journal Constitution* (April 14, 2002), F1.

12. Stephen Jay Gould, "In the Mind of the Beholder," *Natural History* (February 1994), 103:14.

13. Sylvester Petro, *The Kingsport Strike* (New Rochelle, NY: Arlington House, 1967), 27–28.

14. See, for example, Rousas J. Rushdoony, *The Institutes of Biblical Law* (Phillipsburg, NJ: Presbyterian and Reformed, 1973), 541; Russ Walton, *One Nation under God* (Nashville, TN: Thomas Nelson, 1987), 12; D. James Kennedy and Jerry Newcombe, *What If Jesus Had Never Been Born?* (Nashville, TN: Thomas Nelson, 1994), 71; John H. Stormer, *Betrayed by the Bench: How Judge-Made Law Has Transformed America's Constitution, Courts and Culture* (Florissant, MO: Liberty Bell Press, 2005), 5.

15. The case has been made by William J. Federer, *The Ten Commandments and Their Influence on American Law: A Study in History* (St. Louis, MO: Amerisearch, Inc., 2003) and at http://www.eppc.org/docLib/20050204_decalogue.pdf

16. Bishop James Madison, *The Virginia Gazette* (September 18, 1779): http://www.loc.gov/loc/madison/hutson-paper.html

17. http://www.jmu.edu/centennialcelebration/HU.shtml

18. For example, W. David Stedman and LaVaughn G. Lewis, eds., *Our Ageless Constitution* (Asheboro, NC: W. David Stedman Associates, 1987), 263.

19. http://www.lib.ed.ac.uk/faqs/parqs.shtml#Aftytler2

14

History As Theater

"One of the first duties of a man is not to be duped."[1]

FOR MORE THAN a century, school children have been taught the fable by misinformed textbook writers that Christopher Columbus had to defend a round-earth theory against a prevailing flat-earth belief system held by church authorities before his voyage would be approved and funded. In this case, the Bible trumped science as an explanation of how the world was constructed. While this might make good theater, it has no connection with the historical record.

Columbus authority and biographer Samuel Eliot Morison describes this supposed flat-earth debate as "pure moonshine" and "misleading and mischievous nonsense."[2] The nonsense was even immortalized in Ira and George Gershwin's 1936 song "They all Laughed" with the line, "They all laughed at Christopher Columbus when he said the world was round." In reality, no one of any importance in the late fifteenth century believed that the earth was flat, especially since the Church had adopted elements of Ptolemy's (*c*. 100–165) cosmology which definitely proposed that the earth "when taken as a whole [is] sensibly spherical in shape." The debate with Columbus was over how big around the earth was. On this point, Columbus was wrong and the scholars trained in church-established institutions of learning were right.

The Bible and a Flat Earth

Despite the evidence to the contrary, textbook writers continued to perpetuate the myth that the scholars associated with the Church and its academic institutions insisted that the earth was flat based on biblical texts that use language like "four corners" (Isa. 11:12; Ezek. 7:2; Rev. 7:1; 20:8) and "four winds" (Jer. 49:36; Ezek. 37:9; Dan. 7:2; 8:8; Zech. 2:6; Matt. 24:31; Rev. 7:1). The use of metaphors has always been a common feature in literature and science, especially when there was no ready and agreed upon explanation for how things actually worked. Poetic language is common in the Bible, especially when describing the wonders of creation (Job 38:4–11). These descriptions were never meant to be taken literally, and it's my guess that they rarely were.[3] Henry Morris writes, while "there are no scientific mistakes or fallacies" in Job, the book "was not written as a book of science at all."[4] To claim that these metaphors and poetic descriptions were actual depictions of what was going on scientifically is reading today's scientific knowledge into the past. The fallacies of "presentism" and "backward projection"[5] lead to the distortion of the historical record and a misperception of how people consciously struggled to understand God's creation.

Even today scientists write about how inanimate bodies like planets, moons, and stars "obey" certain natural "laws." How can a planet, with no consciousness, "obey a law"?[6] We say that the moon "influences the tides." How is such influence accomplished by an inanimate ball hanging in space? By force of will? We don't think anything of using such language, but put the same descriptive words in the mouth of a sixteenth-century churchman, and he's considered scientifically ignorant and an impediment to scientific progress. Nicholas Copernicus (1473–1543), author of *On the Revolutions of the Celestial Spheres* (1543) was not opposed to using descriptive metaphors to describe the working of the cosmos:

> At rest, however, in the middle of everything is the sun. For in this most beautiful temple, who would place this lamp in another or better position than that from which it can light up the whole thing at the same time? For, is not the sun called "the lantern of

the universe" and "its mind" and by others "its ruler"? Hermes the Thrice Greatest calls it "a visible god," and Sophocles' Electra, "the all-seeing." Thus indeed, as though upon a royal throne, the sun governs the family of planets revolving around it. Moreover, the earth is not deprived of the moon's attendance. On the contrary, as Aristotle says in a work on animals, the moon has the closest kinship with the earth. Meanwhile the earth has intercourse with the sun, and is impregnated for its yearly parturition. In this arrangement, therefore, we discover a marvelous symmetry of the universe, and an established harmonious linkage between the motion of the spheres and their size, such as can be found in no other way.[7]

Notice how the sun, moon, and earth are given personality traits as if they are alive. The sun is not the center "of all." It's more than a "lamp." It's not a "temple," and it's not "seated on a throne." Copernicus uses language that sounds very much like the Bible (see Ps. 18:5–6). Apparently he saw no conflict with the use of metaphors and his more precise scientific terminology, and neither should we.

The Flat Earth Today

Even today we operate in terms of an earth that is observationally flat even though the science of the day tells us otherwise. I doubt that a survey crew takes into account the curvature of the earth on most of its jobs. Pull out the survey map of your property; it's flat with four corners. Families don't take globes with them when they travel, and yet there is no claim that Rand/McNally believes in a flat earth because the maps it sells are all flat representations of the curved terrain of the earth. All maps are flat and have four corners, and they work well enough to get us around the world. Airplane pilots carry flat maps into the cockpit even though their flights take place over curved land. GPS systems project their maps on flat screens.

Let's suppose that 500 years from now, archaeologists dig up the Library of Congress from 100 feet of rubble and dust and find the map room. Will they conclude that we believed the earth was flat after studying the thousands of flat maps they find in the debris? If a time capsule that included an atlas of our world as it exists today were unearthed two thousand years from now, would these future earthlings suppose that we believed in a flat earth? Would they think we believed that the sun revolves around the earth if they found a daily newspaper that reported the exact time when the sun "rose" and "set"? How unscientific! Didn't these editors ever hear of the Copernican Revolution and Galileo's struggle to make his celestial observations known? A more nuanced approach would be scientifically accurate but awkward and unnecessary:

> Consider. If I say, "The sun rose at 6:01 this morning," that statement is perfectly true and communicates perfectly what is meant. I can also say something more precise, like: "At exactly 6:01:49 A.M., Greenwich Mean Time, the horizon of the earth dropped to reveal the upper tip of the sun as observed from 41°14'22.18" latitude and 55° 21' 45.44" longitude." This second statement is more precise, but not more true than the previous one. We understand the first statement perfectly well.[8]

Nobody describes their observation of the sun and moon in these terms, so why do we demand such precision of the ancients? It's time that we give past generations the benefit of the doubt when it comes to scientific discovery. But why is the flat earth myth so hard to exorcise from history texts, popular culture, and its use as a rhetorical club against creationists, Intelligent Design advocates, and those who believe the moral prescriptions in the Bible are applicable today? Those who championed Darwinian evolution in the late nineteenth century saw that by adopting and perpetuating the flat-earth myth they could discredit critics of evolution by claiming that they hold unscientific opinions contrary to observable evidence.[9] The same tactic is used today but with less success.

Monkey Business

A similar retelling of history is evident in the way the 1925 Scopes "Monkey" Trial has been portrayed in the media and textbooks. Most people, young and old alike, have had their opinions about the creation-evolution controversy shaped by the fictional play and movie *Inherit the Wind*. Consider the following comment from *Home Media Retailing* publisher Don Rosenberg who uses "home video to teach lessons to his children."

> With prayer in schools and the creation-evolution debate in the news, he watched *Inherit the Wind*, the 1960 film that starred Spencer Tracey and is based on the Scopes Monkey Trial of 1925, with one of his sons. "If I didn't know this was made in 1960, you would think the dialogue was being said today."[10]

And that's just the problem. The dialog in the movie is not based on what really happened at the trial. It's unfortunate that the real story of the Scopes Trial has been obscured by its fictional counterfeits since it has distorted the historical record almost beyond repair. *Inherit the Wind*, Donald J. Larson writes, "may not have been accurate history, but it was brilliant theater—and it all but replaced the actual trial in the nation's memory."[11] Ronald L. Numbers, author of *The Creationists*, writes that *Inherit the Wind* "dramatically illustrates why so many Americans continue to believe in the mythical war between science and religion."[12]

Despite its less than accurate portrayal of the actual trial, "*Inherit the Wind* became a popular instructional tool for teaching students about the [1920s]. In 1994, for example, the National Center for History in Schools published instructional standards. As a means to educate high school students about changing values during the 1920s, it recommended that teachers 'use selections from the Scopes trial or excerpts from *Inherit the Wind* to explain how the views of William Jennings Bryan differed from those of Clarence Darrow.'"[13] A better academic exercise would have been to compare *Inherit the Wind* with the actual events of the trials.

But like the flat-earth legend concocted by the fictional writer Washington Irving and used by evolutionists to discredit anti-evolutionists, *Inherent the Wind*'s mischaracterization of the events and the central players in the Scopes Trial often obscures genuine attempts to study main points in the creation-evolution debate. Where the classroom should be a welcoming setting for spirited debate on all topics, it has become a controlled atmosphere to eliminate dissent. One of the important points often missed in a discussion of the Scopes Trial is that the defense did not want to stop teaching a biblical view of origins in Tennessee public schools. The goal was to allow for a discussion of alternate theories. It's remarkable that today, the roles have been reversed. It's the evolutionists who will not allow a competing theory in the classroom.

An Uncivil Biology

The biology text used in the Dayton, Tennessee, school system in 1925, was George William Hunter's *Civic Biology* (1914), the best-selling text at the time. Hunter's work was "heavily laced with the scientific racism of the day. According to Hunter, 'simple life forms of life on earth slowly and gradually gave rise to those more complex.' Humans appeared as a progressive result of this evolutionary process, with the Caucasian race being 'finally, the highest type of all.'"[14] Like so much about the trial, the content of Hunter's text is rarely discussed.

The book is not so much a scientific defense of Darwinism but a rehearsal of "Darwinism's social implications. In particular, chapter seventeen discusses the application to human society of 'the laws of selection' and approves the eugenic policies and scientific racism common in the United States at the time.' (Scopes, a substitute teacher planted by the ACLU to test Tennessee's anti-evolution law, was teaching his students from chapter seventeen.) In his *Civic Biology*, 'Hunter believed that it would be criminal to hand down 'handicaps' to the next generation and regarded families with a history of tuberculosis, epilepsy and feeblemindedness as 'parasitic on society.' The remedy, according to Hunter, is to prevent breeding."[15]

Hunter describes the "Jukes" and "Kallikak" families as "notorious example[s]" of bad heredity that resulted in feeble-mindedness, criminality, alcoholism, and sexual immorality. These true societal parasites spread "disease, immorality, and crime in all parts of this country." Hunter sees a logical evolutionary solution, but he believes "humanity will not allow this." On what grounds he does not say. In terms of evolution, stopping the propagation of the Jukes and Kallikaks is logical given evolutionary assumptions about the survival of the fittest:

> If such people were lower animals, we would probably kill them off to prevent them from spreading. Humanity will not allow this, but we do have the remedy of separating the sexes in asylums or other places and in various ways preventing intermarriage and the possibilities of perpetuating such a low and degenerate race. Remedies of this sort have been tried successfully in Europe and are now meeting success in this country.[16]

Evolution validated the eugenics movement by giving it scientific legitimacy. The same was true about entrenched ideas concerning race. Hunter believed that of the "five races or varieties of man" that have evolved, "the highest type of all" is "the Caucasians, represented by the civilized white inhabitants of Europe and America."[17]

Robert Lewis Dabney (1820–1898), a Southern Presbyterian theologian, understood the moral implications of Darwinism when he wrote:

> If mine is a pig's destiny, why may I not hold this "pig philosophy"? Again, if I am but an animal refined by evolution, I am entitled to live an animal life. Why not? The leaders in this and the sensualistic philosophy may themselves be restrained by their habits of mental culture, social discretion and personal refinement (for which they are indebted to reflex Christian influences); but the herd of common mortals are not cultured and refined, and in them the doctrine will bear its deadly fruit.[18]

Because Christianity had so impacted nineteenth-century society, the ethical and cultural effects of Darwinism were at first minimal. In time, however, as consistency began to be demanded of the new naturalistic worldview, the evolutionary dogma impacted the world in ominous ways. Marxism and Nazism are built on Darwin's theory. "Given the close relationship between Darwinism and the horrific crimes committed by Mussolini, Hitler, Stalin, Mao and Pol Pot's Khmer Rouge Regime we are forced to conclude that ours has been the Darwinian century."[19]

Notes

1. Carl Becker (1873–1945). Quoted in David Hackett Fischer, *Historians' Fallacies: Toward a Logic of Historical Thought* (New York: Harper & Row, 1970), 40.

2. Samuel Eliot Morison, *Admiral of the Ocean Sea: A Life of Christopher Columbus* (Boston, MA: Little, Brown and Co., 1942), 89.

3. For example, George Hutcheson, *An Exposition of the Book of Job* (London: Gresham College, 1669).

4. Henry Morris, *The Remarkable Book of Job: The Ancient Wisdom, Scientific Accuracy, and Life-Changing Message of an Amazing Book* (Grand Rapids, Baker Book House, 1988), 48.

5. Fischer, *Historians' Fallacies*, 136–137.

6. There is no better description of this than the chapter on "The Heavens" in C.S. Lewis, *The Discarded Image: An Introduction to Medieval and Renaissance Literature* (London: Cambridge University Press, 1964), chap. 5.

7. Nicholas Copernicus, *On the Revolutions: Nicholas Copernicus' Complete Works*, trans. Edward Rosen (Baltimore, MD: The Johns Hopkins University Press, 1978), Book I, chapter 10.

8. James B. Jordan, *Creation in Six Days: A Defense of the Traditional Reading of Genesis One* (Moscow, ID: Canon Press, 1999), 109.

9. Paul F. Boller, Jr., *Not So! Popular Myths about America from Columbus to Clinton* (New York: Oxford University Press, 1995), 3–6.

10. Mike Snider, "Bonding through DVD," *USA Today* (September 12, 2006), 2D.

11. Donald J. Larson, *Summer of the Gods: The Scopes Trial and America's Continuing Debate over Science and Religion* (New York: Basic Books, 1997), 241. For a helpful summary of the differences between the actual Scopes Trial and its fictionalized retelling in *Inherit the Wind*, see Carol Iannone, "The Truth About Inherit the Wind," *First Things* 70 (February 1997), 28–33 and Marvin Olasky and John Perry, *Monkey Business: The True Story of the Scopes Trial* (Nashville, TN: Broadman & Holman, 2005).

12. Ronald L. Numbers, "Inherit the Wind," *Isis* 84:4 (December 1993), 764. Quoted in Larson, *Summer of the Gods*, 242.

13. Larson, *Summer of the Gods*, 244.

14. George William Hunter, *A Civic Biology: Presented in Problems* (New York: American Book, 1914), 194–196, 405. Quoted in Larson, *Summer of the Gods*, 23–24.

15. Philip J. Sampson, *6 Modern Myths About Christianity & Civilization* (Downers Grove, IL: InterVarsity Press, 2001), 54–55.

16. Hunter, *A Civic Biology*, 263.

17. Hunter, *A Civic Biology*, 196.

18. Robert L. Dabney, "The Influences of False Philosophies upon Character and Conduct," in *Discourses* (Harrisonburg, VA: Sprinkle Publications, 1979), 4:574.

19. F. W. Schnitzler, "Darwinian Violence," *Christianity and Society* 4:3 (July 1994), 28.

15

It Started With Aristotle

Aristotle—not the Bible—taught explicitly that 'everything moves around the earth.' . . . Galileo was condemned, not because the Bible conflicted with observation but because he differed with the church over what authority should be used to interpret it.[1]

WE TEND TO trust fat textbooks written by professional historians who hold academic credentials. Surely they wouldn't make up stuff or leave important details out of the historic record. And while Hollywood does take some liberties with films based on "actual events," most of us believe there is a concerted effort to get the story right.[2] Think again. As we've already seen, there's a lot to be critical of when reporting on the facts of history as presented in history textbooks:

> If you have been brought up to think that history books tell "the truth, the whole truth, and nothing but the truth," it may come as a real shock to learn that this is often not the case. Some history books omit events unfavorable to their own point of view, while twisting the significance of the facts they do present. A great many books contain half-truths, distortions, and much general misinformation, and many others are guilty of perpetuating certain basic myths and legends—events which are simply not true, but which have been repeated for so many years that almost everyone takes them for granted.[3]

This is no more evident than in the way religion and science are portrayed in the history books. Students are being taught that religion and science do not mix. Sam Harris and other New-Atheist advocates believe that religion is a deterrent to scientific discovery and advancement.[4] The New Atheists are counting on government legislation, judicial pronouncements, and the rewriting of history books to propagandize students so they will come to believe that religion has always been at war with science. In reality, "there has been friction among science and virtually every other intellectual endeavor since the appearance of modern science on the scene since around 1600. So it would be surprising if there were not some heated exchanges between science and Christianity."[5] Finding examples of a few battles between religion and science does not make a war. And as we will see, much of the criticism leveled against new scientific theories was due more to the fact that there was no empirical evidence to support them.

A study of the history of science will show that at times science itself has been an impediment to scientific advancement.[6] For example, after Italian biologist Francesco Redi (1626–1697) successfully challenged the dogmatism of spontaneous generation which had been for so long based on Greek "science," some scientists still held to elements of the outmoded theory. Even when additional experiments by Louis Pasteur (1822–1895) showed that "microscopic beings must come into the world from parents similar to themselves,"[7] skepticism remained among some scientists that hindered Pasteur's work. Ernst Haeckel (1834–1919), a chief proponent of Darwinism, stated in 1876, 25 years *after* Pasteur's famous experiment, "If we do not accept the hypothesis of spontaneous generation, then at this one point in the history of evolution we must have recourse to the miracle of a supernatural creation."[8] Haeckel chose spontaneous generation even though there was no empirical evidence to support it because he did not like the alternative—belief in God. Sir James Gray, a leading British zoologist, in a 1933 address before the British Association, put it this way: "The spontaneous origin of living [matter] from inanimate matter must be regarded as a highly improbable event, and as such can be assumed not to have occurred. We conclude, then, that science is unable to put forward any satisfactory explanation as to how life arose in the first place. We must therefore accept the Bible doctrine that God created life, or go on making improbable speculations."[9]

Don't be surprised by Haeckel's irrationalism. Despite the evidence to the contrary, a number of high profile modern-day evolutionists have constructed their theory of origins on the rejected premise that life as we know it today developed (evolved) from non-life. Consider this startling admission by Nobel Prize winner George Wald (1906–1997):

> There are only two possible explanations as to how life arose. Spontaneous generation arising to evolution or a supernatural creative act of God. . . . There is no other possibility. Spontaneous generation was scientifically disproved 120 years ago by Louis Pasteur and others, but that just leaves us with only one other possibility. . . that life came as a supernatural act of creation by God, but I can't accept that philosophy because I do not want to believe in God. Therefore I choose to believe in that which I know is scientifically impossible, spontaneous generation leading to evolution.[10]

The same words coming from the mouth of a theologian would be rejected on the spot. He would be accused of letting his religious assumptions interpret the facts. But when a scientist follows a similar methodology in defense of evolution, hardly anyone blinks a questioning eye because the declaration is made in the name of science.

In addition to not being able to account for biological life within the confines of accepted scientific theory and experimentation, evolutionists are unable to account for the needed information that gives instructions on how an organism functions. It's one thing to postulate that eyes, ears, tongues, and hearts evolved, an impossible task given the inherent problems in partially evolved organisms,[11] it's another thing to explain where the information (programming) came from so these supposed evolved organs will operate properly and long enough to propagate themselves. And how does an organism know what's pertinent to the propagation of its existence, and why would it care? In addition, evolutionists, who are strict materialists (only matter matters), cannot account for the source of the needed information since information does not have the properties of matter. Dr. Werner Gitt, an information specialist, outlines the problem for the evolutionist:

> The question "How did life originate?" which interests all of us, is inseparably linked to the question "Where did the information come from?" Since the findings of James D. Watson . . . and Francis H. C. Crick, it was increasingly realized by contemporary researchers that the information residing in the cells is of crucial importance for the existence of life. Anybody who wants to make meaningful statements about the origin of life would be forced to explain how the information originated. All evolutionary views are fundamentally unable to answer this crucial question.[12]

Consider the computer. Not only must all the physical parts work flawlessly—parts which were designed and manufactured—the programming necessary to run the parts also must function without error. No one would ever propose that the computer evolved spontaneously or that the programming appeared out of thin air and found its way into the computer's internal parts without some form of outside design and directive to operate in a specific way.

Perpetuating Historical Myths

The perception that there has always been a war between religion and science is of recent vintage. The myth finds its most formal statement in the nineteenth-century works of John William Draper's *History of the Conflict between Religion and Science* (1874) and Andrew Dickson White's *History of the Warfare of Science with Theology in Christendom* (1896). White introduces his work with the claim that he is "letting the light of historical truth into the decaying mass of outworn thought which attaches the modern world to medieval conceptions of Christianity and which lingers among us—a most serious barrier to religion and morals, and a menace to the whole normal evolution of society."[13] The view of these two volumes is that when there have been proposals for a new scientific explanation on how the world works, Christians have been the first to condemn them because they conflict with some supposed scientific statement in the Bible and all religiously non-affiliated scientists are the first to accept them because science is "self-correcting"[14] while so-called Christian science is not.

Draper makes the unsupported claim that scientific "opinions on every subject are continually liable to modification, from the irresistible advance of human knowledge."[15] This is hardly true given the nearly maniacal reluctance to test the absolutist claims of modern-day evolutionary theory. For example, "a new report from the U.S. House of Representatives has condemned officials at the Smithsonian Institution for imposing a religious test on scientists who work there. And it suggests their attacks on a scientist who just edited an article on intelligent design are just the tip of the iceberg of an industry-wide fear of anything that suggests man might not have come from a puddle of sludge."[16] In reality, many new scientific theories are often opposed by scientists for any number of reasons. There is continued scientific debate over the causes or even the reality of human-caused global warming, whether oil is a fossil fuel or a renewable abiotic resource,[17] the medical benefits of embryonic stem-cells over against adult stem-cells, and much more. These debates can be downright hostile as charges and counter charges are lobbed from scientific strongholds where the claims are made that there is no room for debate. Consider the Inquisition-like reaction to those who question the certainty of global warming:

> Scientists who dissent from the alarmism [over global warming] have seen their grant funds disappear, their work derided, and themselves libeled as industry stooges, scientific hacks or worse. Consequently, lies about climate change gain credence even when they fly in the face of the science that supposedly is their basis. . . . In Europe, Henk Tennekes was dismissed as research director of the Royal Dutch Meteorological Society after questioning the scientific underpinnings of global warming. Aksel Winn-Nielsen, former director of the U.N.'s World Meteorological Organization, was tarred by Bert Bolin, first head of

the IPCC, as a tool of the coal industry for questioning climate alarmism. Respected Italian professors Alfonso Sutera and Antonio Speranza disappeared from the debate in 1991, apparently losing climate-research funding for raising questions.[18]

Some have gone so far as to propose that "global warming deniers" are aiding and abetting a global holocaust and should be silenced or prosecuted. Australian columnist Margo Kingston "has proposed outlawing 'climate change denial.' 'David Irving is under arrest in Austria for Holocaust denial,'[19] she wrote. 'Perhaps there is a case for making climate change denial an offence. It is a crime against humanity, after all.' Others have suggested that climate change deniers should be put on trial in the future, Nuremberg-style, and made to account for their attempts to cover up the 'global warming . . . Holocaust.'"[20] These arguments are being made by those within the secular scientific community.

There's a new Inquisition in operation. If you don't hold to the agreed-upon theories, then you will not be hired, and if you already have a position, there is a good chance you will lose it if you express your opinion. "In November, 2005 . . . National Public Radio reported that it had talked with 18 university professors and scientists who subscribe to intelligent design. Most would not speak on the record for fear of losing their jobs. One untenured professor at Kennesaw State University in Georgia wrote that talking to NPR would be 'the kiss of death.' Another said, 'There is no way I would reveal myself prior to obtaining tenure.'" Tolerance and an open mind are a one-way street when there might be a science Inquisitor hiding in the academic shadows.

Copernicus and Galileo Upset the Universe

The views of the sixteenth-century Polish astronomer Nicholas Copernicus (1473–1543) led to the upheaval of the cosmological and astronomical theoretical worlds with the publication of his *On the Revolutions of the Heavenly Spheres* in 1543. Elements of a stationary earth and geocentric (earth-centered) solar system, advocated by Aristotle (384–322 B.C.), advanced and refined by the Egyptian Mathematician/Astronomer Ptolemy (A.D. 100–170), and mostly unquestioned for nearly 1900 years, was being reassessed by a number of scientists before Copernicus but without the required mathematical and/or empirical evidence that would overrule in a convincing way what people could see with their eyes and experience with their senses each day.[21]

Many modern-day secular scientists, historians, and textbook writers contend that the church opposed scientific speculations like those of Copernicus because they contradicted the Bible in some way. The true story of sixteenth-century belief systems regarding science is far more complex and thoughtful than most moderns would have us believe. It's unfortunate that the textbooks obscure the truth to score academic and worldview points.

Medieval science as practiced by Christians went astray when "the Bible was . . . read through 'Greek' spectacles."[22] Certainly the Greeks were right in many of their observations and experiments, but the West's almost religious attachment to Greek cosmology was what most impeded scientific advancement. The Greeks, specifically Aristotle, argued for an earth-centered (geocentric) positioning of the universe. Since the Bible says very little about science as compared to what we know today and expresses no comprehensive cosmological theory beyond that God "created the heavens and the earth" (Gen. 1:1), the sun, moon, and stars are not objects of worship (Deut. 4:19; Isa. 47:12–15), and the cosmos operates in terms of fixed laws, it was natural to look at practiced and studied theories that might explain how the heavens operate. Aristotelian cosmology was seemingly a rational choice. Unfortunately, it turned out to be the wrong choice.

Galileo's (1564–1642) struggle to get a hearing for his scientific views is often depicted as a war between religion and science, with the Christian religion being the chief antagonist. Like the Columbus myth, the facts surrounding the Galileo affair are often obscured by an incomplete telling of the story. Giorgio de Santillana, author of *The Crime of Galileo*, "argues that the Galileo affair was not a confrontation between 'the scientist' and a religious credo at all. Ironically 'the major part of the Church intellectuals were on the side of Galileo,' de Santillana notes, 'while the clearest opposition to him came from secular ideas' (i.e., from the academic philosophers)."[23] Galileo's "sin" was that he attacked "Aristotelian philosophy—and all the metaphysical, spiritual, and social consequences" the Church "associated with it."[24] For the most part, the scientific ideology and moral philosophy of the day were based on an Aristotelian cosmology and the Bible as read through Aristotle.

> The reason some churchmen resisted giving up Aristotelian physics and cosmology was because these were intimately tied to an overall vision of moral and social life. If that tie were broken, they feared morality itself would be destroyed. Hence Galileo seemed to promote doctrines that were not only wrong but dangerous.[25]

Aristotle attempted to present a comprehensive explanation of reality without any reference to a personal god. His "unmoved mover" or "first cause" was a principle of existence, not a personal being. It was Thomas Aquinas (1224–1274) who hoped to teach Aristotle to "speak like a Christian,"[26] to harmonize Aristotelian philosophy with Christianity. By the time of Galileo, the views of Aristotle had become the doctrines of the church. So then, it was pagan Greece that led the Church astray, not a supposed flawed biblical cosmology.

It's not that Aristotle was wrong on everything he taught about the universe. When he stuck with observations, he was mostly correct. By observing lunar eclipses and the earth's round shadow that appeared on the face of the moon, he concluded that the earth must be round and not box-like or similar to a four-cornered plate. He also "reasoned that Earth must be round because the sails of a ship come into view before the hull. If the Earth were flat, the entire ship would appear at once."[27] It's when he tried to develop a cosmological system based on *philosophy* that he got himself and the entire western world into scientific trouble.[28]

In Aristotle's cosmology, the orbits of the planets were circular because a circle is the most perfect shape. The heavenly spheres, because they are spheres, were perfect in every way, unlike the earth which is constantly changing and in a state of physical imperfection. "The heavens were eternal and incorruptible, where nothing ever changed—except for comets."[29] These "shooting stars" (meteors) were explained as flashes of light that disappeared as mysteriously as they arrived, therefore they could not be permanent celestial bodies. It was this model of the universe that Copernicus and Galileo disrupted. In terms of observation rather than philosophy, Galileo leveled the first of many blows against the system when he viewed the imperfect surface of the moon through his telescope. The celestial spheres, given Aristotle's theories and not those of the Bible, were said to be perfect, unlike the earth with its many imperfections. If the moon and planets were equally imperfect, then Aristotle was wrong, and if he was wrong on this one observational item, then it was likely that he was wrong on other things as well.

Today's textbooks continue to perpetuate the myth that a Christian worldview was ultimately responsible for impeding scientific progress. In fact, the Church was responsible for accepting the untested Aristotelian science of the day on faith and believing that it was a proper guide to biblical thinking. This was the Church's mistake, and the remedy came when Aristotle's view of the cosmos was finally rejected. As Rodney Stark points out, the truth is, that without a Christian worldview there would not have been the rise of modern-science:

> Real science arose only once: in Europe. China, Islam, India, and ancient Greece and Rome each had a highly developed alchemy. But only in Europe did alchemy develop into chemistry. By the same token, many societies developed elaborate systems of astrology, but only in Europe did astrology lead to astronomy. Why? Again, the answer has to do with images of God.
>
> * * * * *
>
> In contrast with the dominant religious and philosophical doctrines in the non-Christian world, Christians developed science because they *believed* it *could* be done, and *should* be done. As Alfred North Whitehead put it during one of his Lowell Lectures at Harvard in 1925, science arose in Europe because of the widespread "faith in the possibility of science . . . derivative from medieval theology."[30]

Notes

1. Philip J. Sampson, *6 Modern Myths About Christianity and Western Civilization* (Wheaton, IL: Crossway Books, 2001), 39.

2. Frank Sanello, *Reel v. Real: How Hollywood Turns Fact into Fiction* (Lanham, MD: Taylor Trade Publishing, 2003) and Mark C. Carnes, gen. ed., *Past Imperfect: History According to the Movies* (New York: Henry Holt and Company, 1995).

3. L. Ethan Ellis, *40 Million School-Books Can't Be Wrong: Myths in American History* (New York: Macmillan, 1975), 1.

4. Sam Harris, *The End of Faith: Religion, Terror, and the Future of Reason* (New York: W.W. Norton, 2005).

5. Henry F. Schaefer III, "Science and Christianity: Conflict or Coherence?," *Reading God's World: The Scientific Vocation*, ed. Angus J. L. Menuge (St. Louis, MO: Concordia Publishing House, 2004), 124–125.

6. Thomas S. Kuhn, *The Structure of Scientific Revolutions*, 2nd ed. (Chicago: University of Chicago Press [1962] 1970). For a discussion of Kuhn, see C. John Collins, "Thomas Kuhn and Paradigms: A Review Essay," *Science and Faith: Friends or Foes?* (Wheaton, IL: Crossway Books, 2006), 421–433. Also see Dale Ratzsch, *Science and Its Limits: The Natural Sciences in Christian Perspective*, 2nd ed. (Downers Grove, IL: InterVarsity Press, 2000), 38–62.

7. Quoted in J.H. Tiner, *Louis Pasteur—Founder of Modern Medicine* (Milford, MI: Mott Media, 1990), 63.

8. Ernst Haeckel, *The History of Creation*, trans. E. Ray Lankester, 3rd ed. (London: Kegan Paul, Trench & Co., 1883), 1:348.

9. Quoted in John Rendle-Short, *Green Eye of the Storm* (Carlisle, PA: Banner of Truth Trust, 1998), 161.

10. George Wald, "Origin, Life and Evolution," *Scientific American* (1978). Quoted in Joe White and Nicholas Comninellis, *Darwin's Demise: Why Evolution Can't Take the Heat* (Green Forest, AR: Master Books, 2001), 46. "Most modern biologists, having reviewed with satisfaction the downfall of the spontaneous generation hypothesis, yet unwilling to accept the alternative belief in special creation, are left with nothing. . . . To make an organism demands the right substances in the right proportions and in the right arrangement. We do not think that anything more is needed—but that is problem enough. One has only to contemplate the magnitude of this task to concede that the spontaneous generation of a living organism is impossible. Yet here we are—as a result, I believe, of spontaneous generation." (George Ward, "The Origin of Life," *Scientific American* [August 1954], 45, 53. Quoted in Bert Thompson, "The Mythology of Science: Spontaneous Generation" (3): www.apologeticspress.com/rr/reprints/Mythology-of-Science. pdf). In the same article, Wald writes: "We tell this story [about Pasteur's experiments] to beginning students of biology as though it represents a triumph of reason over mysticism. In fact it is very nearly the opposite. The reasonable view was to believe in spontaneous generation; the only alternative, to believe in a single, primary act of supernatural creation. There is no third position." (Quoted in *Life: Origin and Evolution*, ed. C. E. Folsome [San Francisco: W. H. Freeman and Company, 1979]).

11. Michael Behe, *Darwin's Black Box* (New York: Free Press, 1996).

12. Werner Gitt, *In the Beginning was Information: A Scientist Explains the Incredible Design of Nature* (Green Forest, AR: Master Books, [2005] 2006), 99.

13. Andrew Dickson White, *A History of the Warfare of Science with Theology in Christendom* (New York: George Braziller, [1896] 1955), v–vi.

14. Carl Sagan, *The Demon-Haunted World: Science as a Candle in the Dark* (New York: Random House, 1996).

15. John William Draper, *History of the Conflict between Religion and Science* (New York: D. Appleton and Co., 1875), vi.

16. Bob Unruh, "Congress slams Smithsonian's anti-religious attacks: Report documents 'invidious discrimination' in campaign against Darwin dissenters" (December 16, 2006): www.worldnetdaily.com/news/article.asp?ARTICLE_ID=53400. The 29-page report can be read at www.souder.house.gov/sitedirector/~files/IntoleranceandthePoliticizationofScienceattheSmithsonian.pdf

17. Jerome R. Corsi and Craig R. Smith, *Black Gold Stranglehold* (Nashville, TN: WND Books, 2005).

18. Richard Lindsen, "Climate of Fear: Global-Warming Alarmists Intimidate Dissenting Scientists into Silence," *The Wall Street Journal* (April 12, 2006): www.opinionjournal.com/extra/?id=110008220

19. Deborah E. Lipstadt, *History on Trial: My Day in Court with David Irving* (New York: HarperCollins, 2005).

20. Brendan O'Neill, "Global warming: the chilling effect on free speech" (October 6, 2006): www.spiked-online.com/index.php?/site/article/1782/

21. Rodney Stark, *For the Glory of God* (Princeton, NJ: Princeton University Press, 2003), 135–140.

22. R. Hooykaas, *Religion and the Rise of Modern Science* (Grand Rapids, MI: Eerdmans, 1972), xiii.

23. Nancy R. Pearcey and Charles B. Thaxton, *The Soul of Science: Christian Faith and Natural Philosophy* (Wheaton, IL: Crossway Books, 1994), 38.

24. Pearcey and Thaxton, *The Soul of Science*, 39.

25. Pearcey and Thaxton, *The Soul of Science*, 39.

26. Quoted in Mark A. Knoll, *The Scandal of the Evangelical Mind* (Grand Rapids, MI: Eerdmans, 1994), 45.

27. Kenneth C. Davis, *Don't Know Much About the Universe: Everything You Need to Know About the Cosmos but Never Learned* (New York: HarperCollins, 2001), 14.

28. For a discussion of Aristotle's cosmology, see Colin A. Ronan, *Science: Its History and Development among the World's Cultures* (New York: Facts on File Publications, 1982), 103–105 and Angus Armitage, *Copernicus: The Founder of Modern Astronomy* (New York: Dorset Press, 1990), 27–28.

29. Davis, *Don't Know Much About the Universe*, 14.

30. Rodney Stark, *The Victory of Reason: How Christianity Led to Freedom, Capitalism, and Western Success* (New York: Random House, 2005), 14.

The Story of Two Buses

by Gary North

PICTURE THIS. YOU'RE driving down the highway with your nine-year-old son. You're in the middle lane. On your right, one behind the other, are two buses. The bus in front is painted white. The bus behind is painted yellow. The bus in front has its windows painted over. The bus behind does not.

Your son asks you a question. "What are those two buses, Daddy?" You tell him that they are two very different kinds of buses. "How are they different?' he asks. You explain that on the first bus are prisoners who are being taken to jail. On the second bus are students who are being taken to school. "But how is that different?" your son asks. That's what I'm asking, too.

You tell your son that the men on the first bus are required to get on that bus. Then your son asks you if the students on the yellow bus have a choice in the matter. You think about it. Neither group has any choice in the matter. Somebody tells the members of both groups that they must get on that bus and stay on that bus until the bus comes to its destination.

Your son says he doesn't understand. So, you try to make it clear to him. You tell him that the people on the white bus have committed crimes. They are bad people. They are being taken to jail. The people on the yellow bus are good people. They are being taken to school. Your son asks: "Why do they make the good people go on the bus?" That's what I'm asking, too.

Remember, you're talking to a nine-year-old. Nine-year-olds are not very sophisticated. They need clear answers. So, you had better be prepared to provide clear answers.

You tell your son that the good people on the yellow bus are being taken to school for their own good. Your son asks if the people on the white bus are being taken to jail, but not for their own good. No, you tell him. They are being taken to jail for their own good, too. Your son asks, "Then what's the difference?"

The difference, you explain to your son, is that the people on the white bus are very bad and society intends to make them better. Your son asks: "Is society taking the people on the yellow bus to school in order to make them worse?" No, you tell him. Society is taking them to school in order to make them better people, too. "Then what's the difference?"

The difference, you hope to explain, is that the people on the white bus are dangerous people. In order to make society safer, society puts them in jail. The people on the yellow bus are not dangerous. "Then why are they forced to go to a place where they don't want to go?" your son asks. "Because it's good for them," you answer. "But isn't that why the people on the white bus are being taken to jail?" he asks.

You are getting frustrated. You tell your son that they're required to get on the bus because when they are young they don't know that it is a good thing for them to go to school. They don't want to go to school. But they're supposed to go to school. Your son replies that this sounds just like the people in the white bus. But they're supposed to go to jail, you tell him. It's for their own good. They're going to be better people if they go to jail.

Isn't that right? Isn't the whole idea of sending people to jail is to rehabilitate them? Aren't they supposed to become better people in jail? I mean, if they aren't going to become better people, why not just sell them into slavery and use the money to pay restitution to their victims? Why build jails? Why paint buses white?

You tell your son that the bad people have to go to jail in order to keep them off the streets. The problem is, this is one of the reasons why society requires students to go to school. People want to keep the kids off the streets. They want to make certain that somebody in authority is in a position to tell the children what to do. They don't trust the children to make their own decisions. They also don't trust the criminals to make their own decisions.

This is more complicated than you thought. But you keep trying. You explain to your son that bad people must be kept from doing more bad things. Your son asks: "What are the bad things that kids do?" The light comes on. You tell your son that the children are dangerous to themselves, but the prisoners are dangerous to everybody else. The children may hurt themselves, but the prisoners may hurt other people. But your son wants to know why it is that the children must be taken to a school in order to keep them from hurting themselves, when they can stay home and not hurt themselves.

You tell your son that it's because people are not able to stay home with their children. Your son wants to know why not. You explain that both parents have to work to make enough money to live a good life. This means that somebody has to take care of their children. Your son wants to know why parents don't hire somebody to come into their home and take care of the children. Why don't they hire a teacher to take care of them? You explain that it is cheaper to hire one teacher to look after lots of students. Your son wants to know why it's cheaper to send children to school when it costs money to build schools, buy buses, hire drivers, and pay for gasoline.

This is a smart kid.

You explain that the people who have children force people who do not have children to pay for the schools. Your son asks if this is the same thing as stealing. "Isn't that what the people on the white bus did?" No, you explain, it's not stealing. Your son asks, "How is it different?" Now you have a problem. You have to explain the difference between taking money from someone to benefit yourself as a private citizen, which is what a criminal does, and taking money from someone to benefit your-self as a voter. This is not so easy to explain.

You explain to your son that when you vote to take money away from someone so that you can educate your child, this is different from stick-ing a gun into somebody's stomach and telling him that he has to turn over his money to you. Your son then asks if it would be all right to stick a gun in somebody's stomach if you intended to use the money to edu-cate your child. No, you explain, it's not the same. When you tell some-one that he has to educate your child in a school run by the government, it's legal. When you tell somebody that he has to educate your child in a private school, where parents pay directly to hire teachers, it's illegal.

Your son then asks you if it's all right to take money from other peo-ple just so long as you hand over to the government the money to do the things that you want the government to do. You explain that this is correct. "But what if other people don't think that the government ought to be doing these things?" You explain that people don't have the right to tell the government not to do these things unless they can get more than half of the voters to tell the government to stop doing them. Your son sees the logic of this. He asks you: "Are the people in the white bus being taken to jail because there were not enough of them to win the elec-tion?" You know this can't be right, but it's hard to say why it's wrong.

Here is where you are so far. Society makes the prisoners go to jail. It sees these prisoners as dangerous. It wants to teach them to obey. Soci-ety makes children go to school. It sees these children as dangerous to themselves. It wants to teach them to obey. If it can teach both groups how to obey, society expects the world to improve. Society therefore uses tax money to pay for the operation of jails and schools. This in-cludes paying for buses. But there is a difference. Prison buses are white. School buses are yellow.

There must be more to it than this.

So, you keep trying. Schools are run by the government to teach children how to make a living. Jails are run by the government to teach people how to stop stealing. Here is a major difference. "Do they teach prisoners how to make a good living?" your son asks. No, you tell him.

The prison teaches them to obey. He asks: "Then why will they stop stealing when they get out of prison, if they don't know how to make a good living." Because, you explain, they will be afraid to do bad things any more. Your son asks if people in prison learn how to do bad things in prison. You admit that they do. "So," he asks, "we send people to prison and school so that they will learn how to make a good living? Only the difference is, the government pays for a place where bad people teach other bad people how to steal without getting caught, but in school, the government pays good people to teach children how to be good citizens and vote. So, the bad people learn how to steal from the good people without voting, and the good people learn how to steal from each other by voting. Is that how it works?"

That's how it works. Both systems use buses to take the students to school. But the colors are different.

In prison, prisoners sell illegal drugs. Students do the same in school. In prison, the food is terrible. It's not very good in school—possibly prepared by the same food service company. In prison, there are constant inspections. Guards keep taking roll to make sure everyone is present and accounted for. Teachers do the same in school. In prison, you aren't allowed to leave without permission. The same is true in school. In prison, bullies run the show. In school, they do, too. But there is a difference. Prison buses are white. School buses are yellow.

This is too extreme. The systems are different. Criminals are convicted in a court of law before they are sent to jail. Students, in contrast, are innocent. Some prisoners can get parole. The average term in prison for murder is under ten years. Students are put into the school system for twelve years. There is no parole.

Be thankful you are not in one of those buses, either white or yellow.

Index

FOR MORE INFORMATION, PLEASE CONTACT:

P.O. Box 220
Powder Springs, GA 30127

Toll Free (Orders only please):
800-628-9460

Business Office: 770-222-7266
Fax: 770-222-7269

Email: mail@americanvision.org

Website: www.AmericanVision.org